Feet of Clay

Facing Emotions That Make Us Stumble

Paul W. Powell

SMYTH&HELWYS
PUBLISHING INCORPORATED MACON, GEORGIA

Smyth & Helwys Publishing, Inc.
6316 Peake Road
Macon, Georgia 31210-3960
1-800-747-3016
©1999 by Smyth & Helwys Publishing
All right reserved.
Printed in the United States of America.

Paul W. Powell

The paper used in this publication meets the minimum requirements of
American National Standard for Information Sciences—Permanence of
Paper for Printed Library Materials.
ANSI Z39.48–1984. (alk. paper)

Library of Congress Cataloging-in-Publication Data

Powell, Paul W.
      Feet of clay: facing emotions that make us stumble/
      Paul W. Powell.
      Includes bibliographical references.
      pp.   cm.
      1. Emotions—Religious aspects—Christianity.
      2. Emotions—Biblical teaching.
      3. Bible. O.T.—Criticism, interpretation, etc.
      I. Title.
      BV4597.3.P65 1999
      248.4—dc21   98-30882
                                                          CIP

ISBN 1-573132-196-7

Contents

Preface

Some Christians I know have more hang-ups than a hat rack. That used to bother me. But the more I studied the lives of the heroes of the faith, the more I realized that none were wholly holy. They all had their problems.

Longfellow was right: "Some must lead, some must follow, but all have feet of clay." Abraham, the father of faith, doubted God, took matters into his own hands, and had an illegitimate son by his handmaid Hagar. Moses, the meekest man who ever lived, lost his cool and thus lost his opportunity to enter the promised land. The patience of Job wore thin, and he complained bitterly to God. Elijah, the iron man of the Old Testament, became depressed. Solomon, the wisest man who ever lived, played the fool over women.

Even the best of humans are imperfect. Even those chosen by God for places of leadership in God's redemptive work have weaknesses and shortcomings. God's people of all ages experience the same emotions, fight the same battles, and struggle with the same problems.

In this book we meet God's people of other ages on the turf of our common emotions and learn how to keep our feet planted on solid ground. Read on, and you will see.

Depression

Life under the Juniper Tree

Depression is the common cold of our emotions. Eventually it touches everyone—even God's people. It would be nice to think we Christians didn't have dark days, that discouragement came only to those around us. But in reading the Bible, it is clear that the great saints—people we laud as heroes—had times of despair. If we are to experience victorious living, we must, therefore, learn how to deal with depression.

A classic example of a depressed person in the Bible is the prophet Elijah. Elijah lived and served during the days of the wicked king Ahab and his sinister queen, Jezebel, who introduced pagan worship in Israel. He was the champion of orthodoxy, chosen by God to challenge the king and the prophets of Baal and to call the nation back from apostasy. In a contest on Mount Carmel, he was God's instrument to prove to Israel that Jehovah was the Lord. But after that amazing victory, Elijah sank into the depths of despair. He sat down under a juniper tree and asked God to take his life. Does that surprise you about a person of faith? I hope not.

These two experiences, Elijah on Mount Carmel and Elijah under the juniper tree, are set side by side in the Scripture (1 Kgs 18–19), perhaps to show how close we all live to the edge. In chapter 18 Elijah is at the height of success; in chapter 19 he is in the depths of despair. In chapter 18 he is on the mountaintop of victory; in chapter 19 he is in the valley of defeat. In chapter 18 he is elated; in chapter 19 he is deflated. We are all capable of such roller-coaster emotions.

Chapter 18 records the incredible story of Elijah on Mount Carmel. He assembled the people of Israel on the mountain and accused them of spiritual schizophrenia. They could not decide whether to worship God or Baal.

So Elijah challenged the prophets of Baal, 450 of them, to a theological shoot-out. "I'll call on my God," he said, "you call on Baal, and let's see which one answers with fire from heaven. The one that does will be the God of Israel" (18:24).

Baal's prophets accepted the challenge, set up their altar, and began crying to their God. But no fire fell.

"Maybe he can't hear you," Elijah said. Then he suggested that they shout louder. They did, but still no fire fell. "Is he asleep?" Elijah taunted. "You had better wake him up" (18:27).

As a final appeal, Baal's prophets slashed themselves with knives, but that didn't work either. No fire came. Elijah then built an altar, dug a trench around it, and ordered that water be poured over it until the sacrifice was soaked through and through and the ditch around it ran over. Then Elijah prayed a simple prayer. God sent fire to consume the sacrifice, the altar, and even the water.

With that turning point, the people worshiped the Lord and shouted, "The Lord indeed is God; the Lord indeed is God" (18:39). It was a high hour. Everyone knew God's hand was upon Elijah.

Elijah was not permitted to relish the mountaintop experience long, however. As soon as queen Jezebel heard what had happened, she sent Elijah a message saying, "You have killed all of my prophets, and by this time tomorrow, I am going to kill you also" (19:2).

When the prophet of God read Jezebel's message, his heart sank, and he began to run for his life. He ran all the way to Beersheba, the southernmost city in Judah. Beersheba was the end of civilization. Beyond it there was nothing but desert. He was getting as far away from the queen as possible.

There he left his servant, perhaps because he didn't intend to come back, perhaps because he didn't want his servant to see what he was really like. Then he went another day's journey into the wilderness alone. Have you ever gotten so depressed that you didn't want anyone to see just how down you were? Psychologists call it "withdrawal."

When Elijah finally quit running, he sat down under a juniper tree and asked God to let him die. "I've had it, Lord," he said. "Take my life for I am no better than my ancestors" (19:4). They had been unsuccessful in stamping out apostasy in Israel, and so had he. He felt like a failure. He had done his best, but he hadn't succeeded any more than they had. Then, out of sheer physical exhaustion, Elijah fell asleep. He was physically drained and psychologically wrung out.

After a time the Lord sent an angel who prepared a meal for Elijah, awakened him, and gave him food to eat and water to drink. Then he slept again. Once more the angel awoke him and fed him in preparation for a journey to Mount Horeb where he could get away from the people and pressures that were troubling him. Strengthened by the food, Elijah finally reached his destination, 150 miles to the south. This time he had gone as far away from Jezebel as he could go and still be on the same continent.

There he sat down in a cave, wrapped himself up in self-pity, and bewailed his fate. While he sat in dark solitude God asked him, "Elijah, what are you doing?" (19:9). Elijah then told God his sad tale.

> I have been very zealous for the Lord, the God of hosts; for the Israelites have forsaken your covenant, thrown down your altars, and killed your prophets with the sword. I alone am left, and they are seeking my life, to take it away. (v. 10)

Elijah was having a pity party. All of us get down like that sometimes—businesspeople, ministers, homemakers, teenagers. We know people in our offices and homes who are down. At times we all feel ourselves pulled down.

Elijah's depression wasn't bound up in any one cause. Rather, it stemmed from a number of things. There were at least four causes of his depression: fear (v. 3), failure (v. 4), fatigue (v. 5), and futility (v. 10).

Frightened by the threats of Jezebel, Elijah ran for his life. Fear is almost always a factor in depression. Many times, like Elijah, we become afraid of failure, loneliness, not getting a job completed, not making it through school, or not having our marriage go the way we would like for it to go.

Fear comes from Satan—Pray don't panic.

Elijah held a negative opinion about himself. He felt he was no more successful in checking the nation's apostasy than the prophets who had served before him. It's easy to think: "I'm no good. I'm incompetent. God made a mistake when he made me." Elijah was also emotionally drained and physically exhausted. Mountaintops can leave us that way. He needed rest and relaxation. Depression is always related to or reflected in our physical condition.

A sense of futility overwhelmed Elijah: "I am the only one left, and now they are out to get me." He felt alone, hopeless, and had negative expectations about the future. Elijah was looking at life through dark-colored glasses. He saw no way out.

Have you ever felt like Elijah? Perhaps you are feeling like him right now: afraid, alone, exhausted, burned out, and hopeless. If so, you are a good candidate for the juniper tree. I want you to see what helped Elijah climb out of the valley of despair and go on to a lifetime of useful service. It can help you, too.

Someone called the Bible "the manufacturer's operational manual." It is. If you will follow its instructions, life will run smoother for you. In it, through the experience of Elijah, God gives us some divine principles for dealing with depression.

Fortunately, we are not the helpless victims of our emotions. We don't have to be highjacked by our attitudes or by the circumstances of life. We can bounce back from depression to live useful, happy lives. Consider some adjustments that helped Elijah.

Take Time Off

Elijah took time off so he could get physically and emotionally rejuvenated. He had been so busy taking care of the needs of the nation, he had neglected his own needs. He had become physically exhausted and emotionally drained.

When we use up our physical energy, we become exhausted. When we use up our emotional energy, we become depressed. We must therefore find some way periodically to replace the emotional and physical energy that life and work drain from us. If we do not, we will experience burn-out and depression. Elijah needed rest, food, and relaxation. He needed to get away from the people and pressures that were getting to him. So do we occasionally. This poem says it best:

> If you put your nose to the grindstone rough
> And hold it there long enough,
> For you there will be no such thing
> As a bubbling brook or birds that sing.
> These three things will your life compose,
> Just you, the stone, and a ground-down nose.

No one can run full throttle all the time. We need to slow down to an idle occasionally. Some people say it is better to *burn out* than to *rust out*. That's nonsense. It is better to *live out* your life in victory. Getting away helped Elijah. It will help us, too.

There is a close relationship between our physical and emotional state. The body and soul live so close to one another that they tend to catch each other's diseases. If we are down emotionally, it affects the way we feel physically. If we get sick physically, it affects our emotions. Keeping healthy in general—eating the right kinds of food and getting enough sleep and exercise—while no guarantee against depression, may help to prevent it and will certainly keep the body in a better state to deal with it.

So if you are depressed, get a good physical checkup to see if there is anything physically or chemically wrong. If everything is all right physically, take some time off to let your body and soul catch up with one another. Live a balanced life. Establish a rhythm between work and rest. If you don't find it, you will become either a basket case or a casket case.

Let It All Out

In addition to getting rest, Elijah talked through his frustrations. While he sat in a cave feeling sorry for himself, God asked, "What are you doing here, Elijah?"

Have you noticed in Scripture that God is always asking questions God already knows the answer to? God asked Adam, "Where are you?" God knew where Adam was. God inquired of Cain, "Where is your brother, Abel?" God knew that Abel was already dead. God asked Moses, "What is that in your hand?" God knew that Moses had a staff in his hand. Similarly, God asked Elijah, "What are you doing here?" God knew what Elijah was doing there. God helped him get there.

Why, then, did God ask Elijah this question? To get him to think through his situation and then to give him an opportunity to talk, to vent his frustrations. Then God listened nonjudgmentally as Elijah poured out his feelings of anger, bitterness, and self-pity.

We all have such feelings at times. Unless we rid ourselves of them, they will poison us emotionally. There are some health-giving emotions such as love, faith, and hope. But there are also some destructive emotions. Fear, anger, worry, bitterness, hatred, jealousy, and self-pity are slow killers. We must find some way to rid ourselves of these destructive feelings.

But how can we rid ourselves of these pent-up feelings? Exercise, just plain hard work, is one way. It relieves a lot of tension. Some even believe that the brain produces its own "mood-elevating" chemicals that are enhanced by exercise. But exercise, like other activities, is not appealing when we are depressed. We don't feel like doing anything. It's hard enough just to get through the day. At those dark times we lack energy.

Tears are another way. Depressed people tend to cry a lot. That is good. Tears are a God-given way of release. I hope you never lose your ability to cry. Someone has said that the answer to all of our emotional problems is salt water: sweat, tears, or the ocean. There is some truth there.

But talking is perhaps the most effective way to rid ourselves of harmful emotions. When we talk, it is like pulling the plug out of the bathtub. All sorts of bad feelings are drained from us.

The head of the medical school at the University of Oregon said that probably more good is done between two friends at ten o'clock in the morning over a cup of coffee than in the doctor's office all day long. Talking to a friend can help bring life back into perspective and enable us to solve our problems. Everyone needs someone in whom to confide. If we had more friends, we would need fewer psychiatrists. So find a nonjudgmental listener, and pour your soul out to that person.

And as you talk to others, don't forget to talk to God. God will listen nonjudgmentally. Elijah practically accused God of infidelity. But God is not defensive. God deals patiently and tenderly with an overwrought child. Say what you want to God; God can take it. God will not condemn you as you pour out your hurts.

But a word of caution: be careful about dwelling on your problems. If you pity yourself and bore others with repeated stories of your troubles, you will find yourself left alone.

Get Life Back in Perspective

After talking through his frustrations, Elijah gradually put his life back in perspective. He felt that he alone remained faithful to the Lord. His reasoning went something like this: "Here I am doing my best to serve the Lord, and look what happened. God has forsaken me. I alone am left. It's me against the world."

Depressed people often feel like that. They have problems because they pay more attention to negative events than to positive ones, and they focus on the immediate rather than on the long-term consequences of behavior.

Unfortunately, Elijah had arrived at the wrong conclusions. So the Lord revealed just how warped and distorted his view of things had become.

Ultimately, all depression can be traced back to some distorted view of life. Elijah had a distorted view of himself and of God. He needed to know that God was there and that there were others who had not bowed to Baal.

First, God revealed Himself to Elijah in a new and fresh way. God sent a tremendous wind, a cyclone, that ripped through the

Satan doesn't want us to ask questions, we all have doubts.

mountain, but God was not in the wind. Next, God sent an earthquake that shook the whole mountain, but the Lord was not in the earthquake. Then God sent fire and lightning, but God was not in the fire. Finally there came a still small voice through which God spoke. (The Hebrew expression "still small voice" literally means "a voice of low whispers.")

Elsewhere in the Old Testament wind and fire and earthquakes are often manifestations of God. But here God speaks to Elijah in a low whisper. It is as if God is saying, "Just because I have not spoken to you as I have to others in days gone by doesn't mean I'm not here." God wanted Elijah to know that, in spite of the silence of heaven, God was not absent. Jezebel was thundering, but she was not in control. God was quietly going about divine work.

God is the God of wonders, but God is also the God of whispers. Elijah not only needed a new perspective of God; he needed a new perspective of himself. He thought he was the only one who was still faithful to God. God had to remind him that he had seven thousand prophets who had not yet bowed their knees to Baal.

Elijah thought he was more important than he really was. He thought everything depended on him. We sometimes feel the same way. Take note, if God's work depends solely on you and me, God is in serious trouble.

When I become overly impressed with my own importance, I try to think what would happen if a group of women were playing bridge one afternoon and the phone rang, and the hostess was told, "Have you heard the news? Paul Powell just died." When she broke her news to her bridge partners, one of them would probably say, "Oh, that's a shame. He was such a nice man. I really liked him . . . whose bid is it?"

Keep life in perspective. We can't take God's work too seriously, but we can take ourselves too seriously. Not one of us is indispensable. The workers die, but the work goes on.

If I am a beliver am I beliveable?

Get Back in the Mainstream

When Elijah put his life in perspective, he was able to work again. God allowed him to sit in the dark cave of self-pity just so long, and then told him to get up and get busy. There was a new king of Israel and a new prophet to succeed him to be anointed. The time for complaints and self-pity was over. Elijah needed to get back to work. He needed the tonic of a new task.

With us, as it was with Elijah, the best way to quit feeling sorry for ourselves is to start feeling sorry for someone else.

Psychiatrist Karl Menninger was once asked by a Tucson, Arizona, newspaper reporter, "Suppose you think you're heading for a nervous breakdown. What should you do?"

Most of us would have expected the great psychiatrist to say, "See a psychiatrist." But he didn't. Instead his reply was, "Go straight to the front door, turn the knob, cross the tracks, and find somebody who needs you."

Don't sit around in isolation. Don't get all wrapped up in yourself. Get back in the mainstream of life working for God and the kingdom. In helping others we help ourselves.

* * * * *

Elijah whipped his depression and went on to a lifetime of useful service. And so can you. Elijah closed out his ministry in a blaze of glory as God carried him into heaven in a whirlwind and a chariot of fire. Interestingly, the man who wanted to die was one of only two people in the Bible who never died.

Despair need not be the doxology of life. It can be the invocation as it was for me. My prayer for all of us is this: May these dark days make us tender enough to keep focusing on God.

The armor of God is only on the front side. You have to face things to be covered. Turn and run and you are uncovered.

Elijah Depression/Me

God is with us even in the middle of depression.

Even a great prophet like Elijah can become depressed

He will provide for us what we need.

We need to listen for God's small, quiet voice in the whirlwind of stress and fear.

You need not to go through depression by yourself.

Inferiority

I Ain't Nobody's Nothing

In an imaginary conversation between two fallen angels one asked, "What do you miss most about heaven?" He replied, "The trumpet call in the morning."

The trumpet call to action comes not only to angels in heaven; it comes also to people on earth. God does not save us to sit, and soak, and sour. God saves us to serve. So, to every one of us the call to service comes sooner or later. And when it does, we must either answer its summons or find some way to excuse ourselves.

The response we make depends, to a large degree, on how we feel about ourselves. If we have a poor self-image, if we suffer from an inferiority complex, we may say no to God and ultimately miss out on the best.

Moses is a case in point. Moses was born the son of Hebrew slaves in Egypt at a time when the slave population was growing so rapidly that it posed a threat to the national security. Pharaoh ordered all male babies to be put to death, but Moses' mother, believing God had a special mission for her son, refused to obey Pharaoh's edict and hid her child in a basket among the reeds of the Nile River.

The child was found and adopted by the daughter of Pharaoh. The princess sought a Hebrew slave to raise the young child, and in the providence of God, Moses' own mother was chosen for this responsibility.

When Moses grew older, he moved to the palace and was schooled in all the wisdom of Egypt. One day he saw an Egyptian taskmaster abusing a Hebrew slave, so he took the side of his own people and killed the Egyptian. It was an effort on Moses' part to lead a slave rebellion against the Egyptians, but the people refused to follow him. He was forced to flee Egypt, a fugitive from justice.

Moses traveled to Midian where he married a woman and went to work for his father-in-law tending his sheep. While working on the backside of a mountain one day, he saw a bush burning, but it was not consumed. He walked over to see why.

God spoke to him from the burning bush, identifying Himself as the God of Abraham, Isaac, and Jacob. God then told Moses he was chosen to lead the children of Israel out of bondage.

Moses immediately began to make excuses. He replied, "Who am I that I should bring the the Israelites out of Egypt?" (Exod 3:11). "If I go to the children of Israel, they will ask, 'Who sent you?' and what shall I say to them?" (3:13). "Besides," he said, "if I go, they will not believe me" (4:1). Then Moses reminded the Lord that he was slow of speech and would not be the person to try to speak to the most powerful ruler on the face of the earth. God should definitely send someone else.

I must point out in all fairness, however, that Moses' reluctance to answer God's call was not rooted in a rebellious spirit, but in an inferiority complex. Moses felt inadequate, afraid, and handicapped. He simply did not believe he was equal to the task.

That's understandable. He was born a slave. In a sense, he was born in the ghettos. Where you grow up and your family background color your self-image. Moses had already tried once to deliver the children of Israel and failed. Our record of early successes and failures in life affects how we see ourselves. Moses had a speech impediment. Any handicap or peculiarity that causes people to notice us and make fun of us determines how we feel about ourselves.

Moses is a classic case study of a person with an inferiority complex. It can be seen clearly in the excuses he made. One by one God answered those excuses until Moses agreed to do what God wanted him to do. He went to Egypt and led Israel to the promised land. Today he is recognized as one of the greatest persons of God of all ages. Answering God's call did not come easy or automatically for

Moses. He had to deal with his fears and negative attitude and handicap before he would commit himself to God's will.

Some of you feel like Moses today. You feel inadequate, afraid, inferior. You need a new and deeper self-appreciation. You need a new understanding of God. You need to see yourself through Moses' experience and see God's resources.

Moses' experience is related in Scripture for our benefit. There are four marks of an inferiority complex that stand out in the life of Moses. Look at them to see how an inferiority complex affects us and how God helps us deal with and overcome it.

I'm a Nobody

Moses' first excuse was that of insignificance. He felt like a nobody. "Moses said to God, 'Who am I that I should go to Pharaoh, and bring the Israelites out of Egypt?' " (3:11).

Moses looked at his life and saw nothing of competence in himself to do the great work God had called him to do. So his response was, "God, you've got to be kidding. I'm a nobody."

Mark the question Moses asked: "Who am I?" There is something more than humility there. There is in it a tone of self-depreciation, which is always a mark of an inferiority complex.

Moses had not always felt that way about himself. Earlier in his life he had been bold and self-confident. He attempted to lead a revolution on his own by killing an Egyptian. But that attempt had failed miserably, and he fled Egypt in fright. His soul was scarred. Gone was the old self-sufficiency that once marked him. He had moved from pride to humility to self-debasement. He no longer saw anything of worth in himself to do the great work of God.

The question "Who am I?" is one of the three great questions of life. The other two are: "Why am I here?" and "Where am I going?" The first is a question of identity; the second is a question of meaning; and the third is a question of destiny. We can never be fully satisfied until we have an adequate answer to each of these questions.

The Word says we are created to glorify God and our destiny is Heaven.

In many ways the question of identity is the most important of the three. At the heart of it is our self-image. If we ever feel about ourselves as Moses felt about himself, we are in danger of settling down to mediocrity in Midian and doing nothing but existing.

We must be careful about forming our self-image too soon. If we do, we might make a terrible mistake. I have a friend whose college roommate's first date was with Billy Graham. When she arrived home from her date, her father was waiting up for her and said, "Honey, I don't want you to have anything else to do with that Graham boy. He's never going to amount to anything."

What if Billy Graham had overheard that remark and believed it? It might have colored his self-image for the rest of his life and kept him from making himself available to God to be used in such a marvelous way.

Richard Rhodes, in his sketches of Dwight D. Eisenhower, tells how in his early years Eisenhower was a rebel against all authority. He hated school, had a violent temper, and was continually in hassles with his brother. Then Rhodes added, "Men of destiny are often hard to tell from other men."

So, be careful about writing yourself or others off too soon. Who knows what God might have in store for the "nobodies" of life? Besides, self-depreciation is inconsistent with true faith in God. If God created us, redeemed us, indwells us by the Holy Spirit, and calls us into service, then it is not right that we depreciate ourselves and doubt God. We are somebody!

Moses focused on his own weakness rather than on God's strength. To bolster his sagging spirit, the Lord said to Moses, "I will be with you" (3:12). The same promise is made to us. So the issue is never "Who am I?" but "Who is God?" If God is with us, strengthening and enabling us, we are somebody. We are adequate. Knowing and remembering this will diminish our feelings of inferiority.

I'm Ignorant

Moses' second excuse was ignorance. He was afraid the people would ask him a question he couldn't answer. Moses said to God,

> If I come to the Israelites and say to them, "The God of your ancestors has sent me to you," and they ask, "What is his name?" What shall I say to them? (3:13)

Moses said in essence, "Okay, God, suppose I go to Egypt and tell the people you sent me. As sure as I do, the people will ask me your name. And, God, I don't even know your name."

Moses' fears had some basis. The Hebrews had been in slavery so long, they had lost contact with their ancestral faith. They didn't know God.

Moses feared the people would ask him a question he couldn't answer, which would expose his ignorance. He was afraid he would be embarrassed. Fear of embarrassment is always a part of an inferiority complex.

We will do almost anything to keep people from thinking we don't know everything. Why should we be ashamed of our ignorance? After all, we are all born totally ignorant. Mark Twain once described a man as being as ignorant as a newborn babe. In fact, he said, "He was as ignorant as twins."

Neither time nor education solves the problem completely. Will Rogers' classic observation was right: "Everybody is ignorant, only on different subjects."

Life is, in reality, a process of driving back the boundaries of our ignorance and filling them in with knowledge. For example, we often say that Columbus discovered America. But any school kid knows this is not true. A million people were living here before 1492. What Columbus discovered was the ignorance of the rest of the world. He didn't discover America, anyway; he just found it. He didn't discover the wealth of it, the richness of it, the vastness of it, nor the potential of it. Every second and third grade child in school discovers more about America than Columbus ever dreamed.

To alleviate Moses' fear, God gave him a name that expressed the essence of his being. "You shall say to the Israelites, 'I AM has sent me to you' " (3:14).

"I AM" is a strange name for God, isn't it? What does it mean? The name literally means "I am the one who is," emphasizing the dynamic and active self-existence of God. The Lord used this title to convey God's eternity. God thus identified Himself as the eternal, the self-existent, the unchanging one. God said to Moses, "Tell the people that the eternal God, the God who was, the God who is, and the God who evermore shall be has sent you."

So, for Moses' ignorance God gave him knowledge, an answer, and a name. By the way, there is no evidence that anyone ever asked Moses "the" question. Most of our fears are never realized. They are imaginary. But if we yield to them, they can paralyze us into inactivity.

I Might Fail

Moses' third excuse was insecurity. He was convinced he would fail because the people would not believe him. Moses said, "But suppose they do not believe me or listen to me, but say, 'The Lord did not appear to you' " (4:1).

Moses was a negative thinker. He was sure that if he went to the people, they would not believe God had appeared to him. He knew he wouldn't be able to convince them of it.

Again, there was some basis for Moses' skepticism. The Israelites had been in bondage for four hundred years. They had long been demoralized by slavery. And Moses was fully aware of the fact that he had no credentials to recommend him.

By focusing on failure, Moses was whipped before he started. When we are sure we will fail, we don't try; and if we don't try, we surely will fail. It is the fear of failure that keeps many people from venturing . . . and thus from succeeding. As Bertram Russell once said, "The most insecure people on earth are those who are forever playing it safe."

We need to be more optimistic. I like the optimism of the man who was asked on one occasion, "Can you speak German?" He replied, "I don't know. I never have tried."

How do you know what you can do until you try? We never test the resources of God until we attempt the impossible. When you try something new, you always run the risk of getting egg on your face. But it has been my experience that egg washes off.

To reassure the doubting Moses, the Lord asked, "What is that in your hand?" (4:2). Moses had his shepherd's rod in his hand. The Lord commanded him to cast it on the ground. When he did, it turned into a slithering snake.

The Lord then commanded Moses to reach down and pick up the snake by its tail. When Moses caught it, it became a rod once more. Then to further reassure doubting Moses, the Lord told him to put his hand in his bosom. When Moses did and took it out again, his hand was leprous. The Lord commanded him to put his hand back in his bosom. When he pulled it out the second time, it was made whole again.

The Lord was showing Moses that he could change things. If he could change a rod into a snake and back again, if he could turn a hand leprous and make it whole again, then he could change the minds and hearts of unbelieving people.

Moses versus Pharaoh was not good odds. But God and Moses versus Pharaoh was something altogether different. When you answer the call of God, it is never you against the world. It is God in you against the world, and that is something else altogether.

Nothing ever takes our Lord by surprise. God's preparation is thorough. God makes provision for the appointed task. The people *did* believe Moses.

Failure is not making mistakes — failure is not trying.

I Don't Have Any Talents

Moses' fourth excuse was inadequacy. He had a speech impediment and couldn't talk very well. Moses said,

> Oh, my Lord, I have never been eloquent, neither in the past nor even now that you have spoken to your servant; but I am slow of speech and slow of tongue. (4:10)

Moses' excuse was, "I am not eloquent. I am not articulate." His plea was, "God, I just don't have the ability. I am handicapped."

I don't recall God inquiring about Moses' ability. Do you? Our availability and dependability are far more important to God than our capability. But that's the way people with an inferiority complex think. They go through life using their weaknesses and inadequacies as excuses for doing nothing.

If Fanny Crosby had focused on her handicap, she would never have written hymns numbering more than 8,000, for she was blinded by an eye infection at 6 weeks of age. If Beethoven had done that, he would never have written his 9 majestic symphonies, 5 concertos for the piano, and numerous sonatas, for he began losing his hearing at age 20 and was stone deaf by 50. If Milton had majored on his physical condition, he would not have given the world *Paradise Lost*, for it was written after he was stricken blind.

The Lord's response to Moses' excuse was,

> Who gives speech to mortals? Who makes them mute or deaf, seeing or blind? Is it not I, the Lord? Now go, and I will be with your mouth and teach you what you are to speak. (4:11-12)

If God made Moses' mouth, surely God could give him the words to speak. We never do God's work by human resources alone. We do God's work in God's power. So don't go through life looking for a handicapped parking space. Give God what you've got, and let God use it. If you will do what you can, God will do what you can't.

Someone Else Can Do a Better Job Lie, Lie, Lie, Lie

Moses was still not convinced. He made one last plea: "Oh, Lord, please send someone else" (4:13). The Lord finally told Moses that his brother Aaron would be his helper or spokesperson. (But once Moses started talking, he filled up the first five books of the Bible before Aaron could hardly say a word.) God had met all of Moses' excuses. For his insignificance, God gave him a promise. For his ignorance, God gave him his presence. For his insecurity, God gave him power. For his inadequacy, God gave him a partner.

Ultimately, the answer to Moses' feelings of inferiority and fear was in God. With all his excuses met, Moses could do nothing but accept the challenge. Reluctantly he went to Egypt. Have you ever known a more unlikely candidate for the ministry than Moses? One of the marvels of the ages is how and why God chooses such people to serve Him.

There is a postscript to this experience that I missed for many years. As Moses journeyed to Egypt, the Scriptures say,

> The Lord met him [Moses] and tried to kill him. But Zipporah [his wife] took a flint and cut off her son's foreskin, and touched Moses' feet with it, and said, "Truly you are a bridegroom of blood to me!" So he [God] let him [Moses] alone. It was then she said, "A bridegroom of blood by circumcision." (4:24-26)

What is the meaning of this strange experience? Obviously, by failing to have his son circumcised, Moses had not obeyed the Lord. Apparently he had discussed this with his wife, and they had had strong words over it. She regarded it as a barbarous act and would not agree to it. On his way to Egypt, Moses was struck with a sudden and near fatal illness, and they both knew why. If he was to lead the covenant people of God, he must obey the covenant himself.

Zipporah, realizing what was happening and why it was happening, reluctantly took a stone knife and performed the circumcision on her son to save Moses' life. She then threw the foreskin down at Moses' feet and said spitefully, "A bridegroom of blood by circumcision."

The point of the experience is this: The one obstacle to usefulness in God's service is not a poor self-image, a lack of knowledge, a negative outlook, or a physical handicap. The one obstacle to usefulness in God's service is disobedience. The one person God cannot use and will not bless is the one who is not obedient.

* * * * *

Someone has said, "If you want to be successful in life, find out which direction God is going, and go with Him." If Moses had refused God's call, he would have missed out on one of the greatest adventures of time and eternity. God would have chosen someone else, and Moses would have been left to chase goats up and down the mountains of Midian. It is the same with us.

We cannot all be great, but we can obey the great God and attach ourselves to great causes. I urge you to do as Moses did and find life at its best.

Bitterness

Rejected, Suspected, and Neglected

At the turn of the twentieth century the storm clouds that had long been gathering in South Africa suddenly broke loose, and Britain and the English-speaking people of South Africa were at war with the Dutch-descended Boers. The *Morning Post* offered Winston Churchill a job as Chief War Correspondent. He jumped at the chance. Once at the front, the troop train on which he was traveling was captured, and he was taken prisoner.

After three weeks Churchill escaped. The first night of his freedom he slept among the empty coal bags of a train. He hid during the day. The second night, as he traveled, he saw the lights of a mining town in the distance. He decided to chance his luck. He knocked on a door. A tall man answered but eyed him with suspicion until he gave his name. "Thank God you have come here," the man said. "It is the only house in twenty miles where you would not have been handed over."

Was it an accident, was it sheer luck, that Churchill knocked on the only door in twenty miles where he could find help? Did it just happen, or was he guided there by an unseen hand? Was God at work in that situation to bring Churchill to the one house where he could be saved, knowing what he would mean to England and to the whole free world during the crucial days of World War II?

Many of us who know the contribution Churchill made to history have no trouble believing that God was at work early in Churchill's life to preserve his life and to bring him to a place of prominence in world affairs. We call this "the providence of God." Providence is the belief that God has a plan for the world and for our lives, working in the affairs of humankind, fitting things together to accomplish the divine purpose. It is belief in the guidance, protection, and control of God to bring God's will to pass.

Churchill's experience is not an isolated case. History, both sacred and secular, is filled with examples of divine providence. The story of Joseph in the book of Genesis is perhaps the most thrilling example in all of literature.

Joseph was the favorite of his father's twelve sons. Unfortunately, his father, Jacob, did not hesitate to show his favoritism. Jacob gave Joseph a new coat and left his other sons to wear hand-me-downs, and he always gave Joseph the easiest jobs around the house. Naturally, the other brothers became resentful.

In addition, Joseph was given to dreams, visions from God, in which he always saw himself ruling over his brothers. One of the problems with dreamers is that they, like joggers and people who get up early, have to tell everybody about it. Joseph told everyone his dreams, which further incensed his brothers. So intense was their hatred of Joseph that one day when they caught him alone and far from home, they threw him in a pit and plotted to kill him. Before they could carry out their scheme, however, they spotted a caravan headed for Egypt. They sold Joseph to the caravan and told their father that he had been devoured by wild animals.

This could have been a devastating blow to young Joseph, who was only seventeen years old at the time. It might have broken his spirit, but he held on to his dream. He kept believing God would accomplish God's purposes. He trusted the providence of God.

In Egypt, Joseph was sold to the captain of Pharaoh's guard. In Potiphar's household Joseph worked hard, and the Lord prospered him. He received promotion after promotion until he was made the overseer of the entire household. He became the top person in the household of one of the top government officials of Egypt.

Joseph had a lot of things going for himself. He was young, handsome, intelligent . . . and always around. That was more than could be said for Mr. Potiphar. He was always away on government business. While he attended to state affairs, his wife fantasized about affairs of her own. It was a typical soap opera situation—an affluent household, a bored wife, an absent husband, a handsome available young man.

On at least two occasions Mrs. Potiphar made sexual advances toward Joseph, but he rejected her. Joseph had such a high regard for his master and such a deep devotion to God, he would not consent. Angered and hurt, Mrs. Potiphar falsely accused Joseph of the very thing he had refused to do. Potiphar believed her trumped-up charges. Acting on perjured testimony and circumstantial evidence, he had Joseph thrown into prison.

Life had handed Joseph a raw deal twice in a row. Surely this would break his spirit. But his confidence in God remained unshakable. His dream would yet come true.

In jail Joseph was a model prisoner and became a trustee. This gave him opportunities to help his fellow prisoners. One of those whom he befriended was the Pharaoh's butler. Before the butler's release, Joseph secured a promise from him that as soon as he was free, he would do whatever he could to help Joseph. But, once released, he promptly forgot his promise. Joseph was left to languish in prison two years longer.

This was enough to break the strongest of people. Joseph had tried to live right, but everything seemed to turn out wrong. He had every reason to be bitter, but his confidence in God remained steadfast. His dream had not faded from his mind.

After two more years in prison, the Pharaoh had a dream he couldn't understand. He called the wise men of his kingdom to interpret it, but no one could. It was then that the butler remembered Joseph could interpret dreams. He told Pharaoh, who quickly secured the release of Joseph and had him brought to the palace. When the dream was related to Joseph, he interpreted it this way: There will be seven years of plenty in Egypt followed by seven years of famine.

Joseph recommended that agricultural reforms be instituted immediately to conserve grain and prepare for the coming famine. Pharaoh was so impressed that he appointed Joseph as his Secretary of Agriculture and gave him vast administrative powers. He was second in power only to Pharaoh. At last his dream had become a

By recognizing God's providence in our lives he take us outside of ourselves.

reality. It didn't happen the way he would have planned it—but it did happen. God had not failed.

In his new position Joseph led the nation in a program of food production and conservation that carried the nation through seven years of the severest famine it had ever experienced.

When the famine came, Egypt became the granary of the world. Caravans streamed there from all parts of the world to buy grain. Among them were Joseph's own brothers. When they appeared before Joseph, he recognized them, but they did not know him. It had been more than twenty years since they had last seen each other. Joseph was a grown man, dressed as an Egyptian official, and all but forgotten by his brothers. It is understandable that they did not recognize him.

When he revealed himself to them, they were frightened. They expected Joseph to be bitter and vengeful toward them. They assumed he would jump at a chance to get even with them. Joseph's response surprised everyone. Instead of seeking revenge, he told his brothers not to grieve or to be angry with themselves, for, he said,

> God sent me before you to preserve for you a remnant on earth, and to keep alive for you many survivors. So it was not you who sent me here, but God: he has made me a father to Pharaoh, and lord of all his house and ruler over all the land of Egypt. (45:7-8)

These words show what sustained Joseph through all his difficulties. It was his confidence that God was working in his life.

With the approval and assistance of the Pharaoh, Joseph moved his father, brothers, and all of their children—about seventy people in all—into Egypt, where they lived in peace and prosperity for the rest of their lives.

In time their father, Jacob, died. Once again Joseph's brothers' old fears surfaced. They thought that maybe Joseph had been gracious to them because of their father. Now that he was dead, they thought Joseph would seek revenge, but Joseph reassured them:

Do not be afraid! Am I in the place of God? Even though you intended to do harm to me, God intended it for good, in order to preserve a numerous people, as he is doing today. (50:19-20)

In these words Joseph acknowledged the providence of God. As he looked back on his life, he saw how the evil intentions of others had been used by God for good. God's providence had overridden their wicked deeds. He saw God at work to accomplish God's purpose. In this case it was to redeem Israel. God had brought Joseph to a place of prominence in Egypt so that he might be a means of saving his whole family.

If ever a person had a right to be bitter and resentful, it was Joseph. But he refused to harbor such feelings. Instead he trusted God to take the wrong done to him by his brothers and turn it into the feeding of Egypt and the very brothers who had sold him into slavery. It was because he saw God as his redeemer in and through all of this that he could keep such a positive spirit about life.

Joseph's life ought to be a source of encouragement and hope to us. If you have been rejected by people you love; if you have been falsely suspected by people you have trusted; if you have been neglected and forgotten by people you have befriended; if you have waited on God, and God has not acted; if you have prayed to God, and God has not answered, don't fling away your faith. There is an overruling providence at work in our lives. If we love, trust, and serve God, our Lord will ultimately bring His purposes for our lives to pass. God can take even the evil intentions of wicked persons and the injustices of life and turn them to good ends.

The experience of Joseph is recorded in Scripture not only to teach us about God's working in his life, but also to teach us about divine providence in our own lives. God is at work in our world, and we dare not miss seeing His hand. If we do, life and its circumstances may very well defeat us.

There are three truths about the providence of God in Joseph's experience that can help us deal with life's bitter experiences.

God's Work Is Not Always Visible

The working of God in our lives is often imperceptible. It is often obscure and difficult to see except in retrospect. Only as we look back are we able to see the hand of God moving in our lives.

There must have been times when Joseph wondered, "Where is God in all of this?" It would have been hard to see the hand of God from the bottom of the pit in Canaan. It would have been hard to feel the presence of God while walking in chains across the desert. It would have been hard to hear the voice of God while languishing in prison in Egypt.

At times he must have wondered, "Why has God forsaken me? What have I done to deserve all this?" In those dark days only his dream and his faith in God kept him going. It was only years later, looking back, that he could say, "God sent me to preserve you a remnant . . . God made me a father to Pharaoh . . . God made me lord of all Egypt."

There is a truth here for us. The working of God in our lives is often unrecognized. It is often so subtle, so veiled, so obscure, that we cannot see it while we are in the midst of it. If we are to see it now, it must be by the eyes of faith.

It is possible to have movement without perception. And it is possible for God to be at work without our seeing it or feeling it. Let me illustrate. The earth is spinning on its axis at a speed of 1,000 miles an hour at this very moment. Yet you and I have no sense of motion. At the same time it is rotating around the sun at a speed of 66,000 miles an hour. Do you feel dizzy? The earth is moving, but we do not perceive it. Einstein used to strike 2 quick blows with his fist in rapid succession and then say, "Between those 2 strokes we travel 30 miles." That's movement without perception. Just so, God is moving in history. God is active in our world and in our lives, even though we don't always see it or feel it.

Someone found the following words scribbled on the wall of a basement in Germany at the close of World War II:

We have to base our knowing that God is with us even we arent sure — Faith not feelings

I believe in the sun, even when it is not shining.
I believe in love, even when I cannot feel it.
I believe in God, even when He is silent.

That's the kind of faith we need—to believe in God when God apparently is doing nothing and saying nothing; to believe that God is working, quietly, secretly, and imperceptibly, implementing His designs, never early, never late, and never in error.

God's Work Is Redemptive

Just as God's plan is often obscure, God is able to take even the wicked intentions and evil designs of others and turn them to good purposes. That's what Joseph saw as he looked back on what his brothers had intended as harm. God had turned that harm into help for thousands.

Joseph put it succinctly: "Though you intended to do harm to me, God intended it for good." The good Joseph had reference to was the redemption of his whole family, the nation of Israel. Joseph's brothers planned to slay him, but God turned their wicked intentions into a means of redeeming them.

Joseph's life is a practical working out of Romans 8:28: "We know that all things work together for good for those who love God, who are called according to his purpose." What this verse does not say is almost as important as what it does say.

It does not say that God causes everything that happens; God doesn't. We must not take everything that happens in life and lay it in the lap of God. To do so is to take the evil of humankind and attribute it to God. God is not responsible for murder, rape, child abuse, or drug addiction. We must not take what the law labels as a crime and call it "the will of God." Nor does Romans 8:28 say that everything that happens is good. It isn't. There is much unmitigated evil in the world today. Neither does the verse say that everything is going to work out for good for all people; it won't. You don't have to move off the block where you live to know people for whom all things are not working out for good.

The promise is only "for those who love God." God can do some things for the person who is walking with Him that God can't do for someone who is running from Him.

Romans 8:28 does not say that all things are working together for good as we define good; they won't. Most often we define good in terms of health, wealth, and success. What is the good promised here? In verse 29 it is defined as a growing conformity to Christlikeness. God dares to take His matchless son as a flawless pattern and make us like him. The will of God for all of us is the same: a maximum family resemblance to our elder brother.

To accomplish this end, God can use all things—the good as well as the bad. God can take the joys of today and the tears of tomorrow, the defeats of one day and the victories of another, and mix them all together for our spiritual good.

No experience has to be a total waste if we give it to God. God has the ability to overrule even the wicked intentions and evil designs of sinful people to accomplish God's glorious purposes. And God will do that in our lives if we love and follow Him.

While there is much evil in the world, both human and natural, that is difficult to understand and accept, there is one thing we can know. God's will is not frustrated by either. God can work in the midst of difficulties and disasters. Divine providence can embrace all experiences—poverty as well as wealth, illness as well as health, failure as well as success. God is not limited. In fact, sometimes illnesses, poverty, and failure are the very tools God uses best to shape and mold our lives. It is our lifestyle.

God's Work Is Progressive

The providence of God not only includes many experiences and circumstances, it also unfolds gradually. It cannot be fully understood until God is through with it.

We are like little children watching a circus parade through a knot hole in the fence. Up ahead there is a band playing beautiful music. Back down the line there are clowns and dancing bears and wild animals. But the only part of the parade we can see is the part directly in front of us. If we could find another vantage point, if we could see from atop a tall building, if we could see the parade in its completeness from beginning to end, it would look so different. But our vision is limited because of where we are. It is so in life. For that reason, we ought not to say that any experience is good or bad until God finishes with it.

If Joseph had evaluated the events of his life while he was in the pit, he probably would have said, "I see no hope." If he had rendered a verdict on life while he was in the courtroom of Potiphar, he probably would have concluded, "There is no justice." If he had assessed his life while he waited in prison in Egypt, he probably would have said, "No one can be trusted." It was only after God was through, as Joseph looked back upon God's finished work, that he could say, "God intended it for good."

We can evaluate an experience too soon. Pat Neff, one-time governor of Texas and later president of Baylor University, told of two schoolteachers who met back on campus after not seeing each other for many years. Their conversation went something like this:

The first woman said to her friend, "I have gotten married since we last met."

The second replied, "Oh, that's good."

The first said, "Well, I don't know about that. My husband is twice as old as I am."

The second replied, "Oh, that's bad."

The first responded, "Well, I don't know about that. He's worth a million dollars."

The second replied, "Oh, that's good."

The first said, "Well, I don't know about that. He won't give me a cent."

The second responded, "Oh, that's bad."

The first said, "Well, I don't know about that. He did build a $200,000 house for me."

The second said, "Oh, that's good."

The first said, "Well, I don't know about that. It burned down last week."

The second said, "Oh, that's bad."

The first said, "Well, I don't know about that . . . he was in it."

The point of the story is, we can't say that something is good or bad until God is finished with it. God's work in our lives is progressive, gradual, and continuous. Therefore, we must not evaluate anything as good or bad by isolated events.

Roger Stauback, the all-pro Hall of Fame quarterback of the Dallas Cowboys, was called by some "Captain Comeback." In his years with the Dallas Cowboys, more than thirty times he brought his team from defeat to victory in the last quarter. Nineteen times it was during the last four minutes, and at least once in the last second of play.

When Stauback was playing, if you gave up and headed for the stadium exit too soon, you might have missed out on the victory. It is the same with life. Don't exit on God until the final gun sounds. If you do, you may miss God's best for you.

The supreme example of what I am talking about happened two thousand years ago. Jesus, the Son of God, came to seek and to save that which was lost. But evil people rejected him and nailed him to the cross. When their work was finished, they brushed their hands and said, "Thank God, that's over. At last we're through with him." Even his friends, when they put his body in the tomb and rolled the stone over the door, thought, "This is the end. It's all over now."

For three long days and nights God seemingly did nothing. The silence of heaven was broken only by the weeping of the angels. But on the third day the angel of God strolled into the garden, rolled away the stone, and the Son of God walked out alive. He has been marching on to victory ever since. The message of the empty tomb is this: "It's not over until it's over."

* * * * *

So, no matter what happens, take heart. If you are in the pit, don't give up. If you are in chains, don't give up. If you have been misunderstood by those you love, if you have been falsely accused, and even forgotten by those you have befriended, don't become bitter or vengeful. If you have prayed and God has not answered, if you have waited and God has not acted, don't despair. If things haven't worked out as you had hoped they would, don't lose heart. Put your life in God's hands. Trust, love, and serve God. Know that God is still working in your life to bring His glorious purposes to fulfillment.

Stress

So Uptight I Twang in a Strong Breeze

In the October 9, 1987, edition of the *Dallas Morning News*, Blackie Sherrod told the following story about Barry Switzer, a former coach of the Dallas Cowboys.

When asked how he handled the pressure of being a football coach, particularly the constant threat of being fired if he had several losing seasons, he said, "Pressure is something some people have to deal with daily, but there are many people who have no idea what pressure is." To illustrate this, he told about his upbringing.

Switzer was born in a shotgun farmhouse outside a dusty mill town in southern Arkansas. The biggest event of his young years came during the summer before the ninth grade, when the REA (Rural Electrification Association) reached down the gravel road where he lived.

"That was a big day for us. It meant we could have running water, indoor plumbing, and even one of those fans to keep us cool on hot nights and keep the mosquitoes away. No more coal or oil lamps and listening to the Grand Ole Opry on a battery radio. Our home wasn't much different from anyone else's. Those were the times, and the times were tough."

Switzer's dad was the county bootlegger. "We were raided many times, and he often spent nights in the county jail. But finally they got serious, and he was sent to the state pen. You can imagine this wasn't kept secret in a small Southern Baptist town. I was beginning to experience what I consider real pressure. Most town folk didn't want their daughters dating the county bootlegger's son."

Switzer's dad got out of prison and returned to bootlegging, and things were almost normal until one night before Barry's senior year at the University of Arkansas when he was awakened by a gunshot. "My mother was a very emotional, depressed, sick woman. I really didn't know how sick she was, or I might have been able to do something. That night in late August she took her life on the back porch." Barry found her and carried her body inside to her bed.

"A few years later, living alone at the old homestead, my dad was murdered," said Switzer. "It was something he and I had discussed and feared might happen. Considering those events, I think I know what real pressure is. The tragedy, the pain, the humiliation, the paranoia, the feeling of being insecure and inferior—I dealt with them. Maybe now you know why I consider myself a mentally tough, thick-skinned individual. Maybe you can understand why the pressure of being fired never bothered me. What happens to me in the future can't be any worse than it has been in the past. But if it is, I'll handle that, too."

Then Switzer added, "Some people are born on third base and go through life actually thinking they hit a triple."

Whether you are born on third base or in left field, stress is a part of every person's life. It is one of those common denominators of life. Punch that clock. Pull that file. Reach that quota. Catch that plane. Meet that deadline. Hurry! Don't wait! That's the kind of pressure and stress we live under today. To live successfully in all of life, and in our Christian life in particular, we must learn to handle stress successfully. If we don't handle it, it will handle us.

Stress is not new, nor is it unique to our generation. People have always faced it. In the life of Daniel and his three friends—Shadrach, Meshach, and Abednego—we have an example of people who lived under great stress and learned to handle it effectively. Their experiences can teach us how to manage our stress.

The story of Daniel and his friends is one of the best known stories of the Bible. From childhood we have thrilled at the story of the fiery furnace and Daniel in the lion's den. But we have seldom thought of the stress they faced in those experiences and throughout their lives.

Daniel was a Jewish lad who, along with some of his other kinsmen, was taken captive at the fall of Jerusalem. He was transported to Babylon, the premier city, the capitol of the most powerful empire that had ever existed up until that time. He lived there for the next seventy years as an example and an influence for God. Because of his noble spirit, Daniel rose from being a captive to being a friend and advisor to kings, and eventually the prime minister of Babylon.

In his rise to become an international figure, in his dealings with temperamental Oriental potentates, in conducting the affairs of state, and in facing the lions' den, Daniel experienced tremendous pressure. Obviously he managed his stress well, for he became imminently successful and lived to a ripe old age.

Daniel's story began in 606 B.C. when Nebuchadnezzar besieged and burned the city of Jerusalem. He sacked the temple, taking the sacred vessels of gold and silver back to Babylon with him. And as was his custom, he chose some of the choice children of Israel, those of nobility with unusual ability and intelligence, and carried them back to Babylon to be trained for civil and diplomatic service in the king's palace.

Daniel was just a lad of fourteen years at the time. He was one of the young people chosen by the king, and privileged in every way. Among other things they ate from the king's provisions, which meant they were served the best meats and the finest wines. There was one problem, however. Some of this food was not kosher. In other words, it was not prepared according to Jewish priestly rules and would include some animals that were regarded as unclean according to Hebrew law.

Deeply devoted to God, Daniel determined he would not defile himself by eating and drinking that which was not kosher. He requested of the prince in charge that he, Shadrach, Meshach, and Abednego be put on a diet of vegetables and water. The prince was hesitant to grant the request, but God brought Daniel into favor with his leader, and the prince agreed to a ten-day testing. The health and appearance of these young men were monitored carefully by the king.

At the end of ten days Daniel and his friends were fatter and fairer than any of the other young men in training. In every way—

physically, intellectually, and spiritually—God blessed the four young men, and the king found them ten times better than all other wise men in his kingdom.

In the second year of his reign King Nebuchadnezzar had a dream that troubled him. He called his wise men to explain its meaning. But when they arrived, the king not only did not know the meaning of the dream, he could not even remember its contents. So they not only had to tell him what the dream meant, but what the dream was. Obviously frustrated, they told the king he was asking the impossible.

The king was furious and threatened to kill all the wise men in his realm, including Daniel and his four friends. When the captain of the king's guard broke the news to Daniel, he could not understand why the king was acting so hastily. He quickly went to the king and asked for more time. With the time granted, Daniel went to Shadrach, Meshach, and Abednego—his prayer partners—and together they asked God for an answer.

When the answer came, Daniel shared it with the king and made sure he understood that God had revealed it to him. The grateful king then acknowledged that the God of Daniel was the God of all gods. Then he promoted Daniel to the office of prime minister of Babylon with authority over all other governmental officials. Daniel remembered his friends and asked that Shadrach, Meshach, and Abednego also be given positions of prominence. The grateful king honored his requests, and they, too, were promoted.

Oriental kings were often vain men who erected statues of themselves and required people to give homage to them. King Nebuchadnezzar made such a statue, a golden image, and commanded the people to bow down and worship it. Anyone who refused would be cast into the fiery furnace.

Shadrach, Meshach, and Abednego, who shared Daniel's deep devotion to God, refused to do as the king ordered. When they were brought before the king and told of their fate, they made a marvelous reply:

Pain of Furnace is short time pain where as deniying God is long term pain.

If our God whom we serve is able to deliver us from the furnace of blazing fire and out of your hand, O king, let him deliver us. But if not, be it known to you, O king, that we will not serve your gods, and we will not worship the golden statue that you have set up. (Dan 3:17-18).

The king was infuriated. He ordered the furnace to be heated seven times its normal temperature and the three young men to be cast in. The furnace was so hot, the executioners burned to death as they threw the young men in. In time the king looked into the fiery furnace and saw not three but four men walking in the midst of the fire. None of them were hurt, and the form of the fourth was like the Son of God. Who was this fourth person the king saw? We cannot know for certain. We only know that it was a divine person who protected the men from the heat.

When they were brought out of the furnace, not a hair on their heads was singed, nor did their coats have the smell of smoke. Once again the pagan king was forced to admit that the God of the Hebrews was the true God.

When Nebuchadnezzar died, he was succeeded by Belshazzar. The new king gave a great feast and invited thousands. The wine flowed freely. Under the influence of alcohol, Belshazzar ordered that the vessels of gold his father had taken from the house of God be brought to him. Then, in defiance to the God of Israel, he drank a toast to the gods of gold and silver, iron and brass, wood and stone.

As he drank there appeared a hand, writing on the plaster of the wall of the banquet hall. The guests became hushed with silence. The king grew pale, worried, and nervous. He sent for his wise men to read the writing, but none could. Then Daniel was brought in to read the message. He gave this interpretation:

God has numbered the days of your kingdom and brought it to an end; you have been weighed on the scales and found wanting; your kingdom is divided and given to the Medes and Persians. (5:26-28).

Their purification turned a nation around.

That night Belshazzar was slain, and Darius the Mede took the kingdom. Darius was a wise and competent administrator. He placed over his kingdom 120 princes. Over these were three presidents, of whom Daniel was first. Everyone reported to Daniel.

Daniel had now served under seven different kings with great distinction and success. But remember, success creates its own stress. Becoming number one is easier than remaining number one. Last year's victories do not suffice for this season's challenges. Meeting last month's quota does not suffice for this month's demands.

There was jealousy in the court. (There almost invariably is). The people under Daniel resented his leadership and popularity and determined to get him. They soon realized that if they found occasion against him, it would have to be at the point of his religion. They developed a plan. They would persuade the king to issue an edict that for thirty days anyone who prayed to any god other than the king would be cast into the lions' den. They carefully drew up the document, took it to the king, and with flattering words persuaded him to sign it. Once signed, according to the law of the Medes and Persians, it could not be changed. Daniel's critics then set a watch over Daniel to wait for the violation.

With full knowledge of the edict, Daniel went into his house where the windows were open in his chamber toward Jerusalem. He knelt down three times a day and prayed and gave thanks to God, just as he had always done.

Daniel was immediately arrested and taken to the king. While the king deeply regretted his action, the law could not be changed, and Daniel was cast into the lions' den. As he enforced his own edict, the king said to him, "May your God, whom you faithfully serve, deliver you" (6:16).

That night the king did not sleep well. He fasted, prayed, and paced the floor. Early the next morning he hurried to the lions' den and called out to Daniel, "O, Daniel, servant of the living God, has your God whom you faithfully serve been able to deliver you from the lions?" (6:20).

We often feel we don't deserve Spiritual Sucess, But God is saying Grace.

Daniel answered that his God had shut the lions' mouths. His accusers were then thrown into the den and devoured by the lions.

Once again God prospered Daniel. He had become a man of international prominence. Daniel lived and served in Babylon from the first year of captivity until two years after the captives had returned. He died at the age of ninety, having served God and humankind with great distinction.

Without being told in so many words, we know that Daniel must have lived a life of tremendous stress. There was the stress of moving from his family, friends, and familiar surroundings. There was the stress of living for God in a hostile, pagan environment. There was the stress of measuring up to the expectations of others. There was the stress of working under seven different rulers. There was the stress of being thrown into the lions' den. And there was the stress of success.

Obviously Daniel handled his stress well, for he lived a long life and was imminently successful in all he did. We can learn some lessons from him.

One of the most important questions in life is, "How can I handle stress so it does not become distress?" I'm not talking about improving our acting ability. We all have the capacity to smile and act calm on the outside while inside our stomach is churning and burning and our back muscles are in knots. I remember years ago a missionary saying to me, "I wish I could be as cool and calm as you are." Little did he know that most of the time I was "so uptight that I twang in a strong breeze."

I have learned much from Daniel since then and want to pass on to you what he teaches us about how to handle stress before it handles us.

Embrace Stress

Stress is a normal part of living; accept it. It cannot, nor should it, be eliminated altogether. Instead, it should be managed. Fiery

By Faith not by sight.

furnaces and lions' dens go with certain jobs. As Harry Truman said, "If you can't stand the heat, get out of the kitchen."

The only complete freedom from stress is death. Humans thrive on stress because it makes life far more interesting. Far from eliminating stress, in some instances it needs to be intensified. Vance Havner said, "You can't play a tune on a limp fiddle string. We need to get wound up about Jesus."

Don't Sweat the Small Stuff

If you embrace stress as a natural part of life, you will more likely learn to accept what you cannot change. If the problem is beyond your control at this time, try your best to accept it until you can change it. It beats spinning your wheels and getting nowhere. Seemingly Daniel and his friends accepted the fact that they must live in the distant land and under hostile conditions. Rather than fretting about it, they accepted it and made the best of it.

Dr. Robert S. Elliot, the man whom one medical journal called "the high priest of stress management," gives some good advice at this point. He knows what he's talking about. He's been there. At age forty-four, Elliot suffered a heart attack while giving a lecture on how to prevent heart attacks. He gives these suggestions:

- Rule number 1 is, don't sweat the small stuff.
- Rule number 2 is, it's all small stuff. And if you can't fight and you can't flee, flow.

More and more everyday I realize the importance of going with the flow because most of what we fret over and sweat over is small stuff.

When Andre Agassi was a seventeen-year-old tennis star, he was named to the U.S. Davis Cup Team. In a television interview following his victory in a major tournament he said, "Jesus Christ has given me the strength and courage to come out and play the way I do. I want to thank him for everything he's done for me. The trophy won't last, and we all know the money won't last. But the Lord will last, and that's something I live for."

Our relationship with the Lord will last, but how many other things are there in our lives creating stress that won't last? Daniel knew that some things must be accepted without complaint. Therefore, there is no hint of his or the three Hebrew children ever fretting over what they could not change.

Take Care of Your Health

Mental health is enhanced by accepting the inevitability of stress and the inability to change certain situations. A good mental state adds to strong physical health, which encompasses a proper diet, rest, and exercise. The king was concerned about the health of the Hebrew boys and saw to it that they had a proper diet.

We need to eat properly. When under stress, nutritional needs increase. This is because our bodies use up food faster during such times. A balanced diet helps us manage stress.

Lack of sleep can lessen our ability to deal with stress by making us more irritable. Most people need at least seven to eight hours of sleep each night. If stress repeatedly prevents you from sleeping, inform your doctor.

And remember, jumping to conclusions, climbing the walls, throwing your weight around, running around in circles, and making mountains out of mole hills won't suffice the requirement for adequate exercise. Stress is energy that needs to be burned up. This energy should be expended through activities that are productive, enjoyable, and socially acceptable—activities such as running, playing tennis, gardening, or walking.

Avoid Cover-Ups

While taking care of your mental and physical health, give attention to your "moral" health. Always do what is right. Cheating, deception, unethical behavior, immorality—all of these can produce guilt feelings, self-condemnation, attempts to "cover up" and, of course, stress. Admit your faults, confess your sins to God, and get into the habit of doing what is right. Daniel did what was right. His friends and foes alike testified that he was a person of honor and integrity.

Seek the Help of Others

Overall health cannot neglect the importance of emotional soundness. We need to develop a network of support. Failure to do this was one of Jimmy Swaggart's mistakes. After his sex scandal he said, "I tried to live my entire life as if I were not human. I thought there wasn't anything I could not do. I think I didn't reach the victory I sought because I didn't seek the help of my brothers and sisters in the Lord."

Learn to talk about your problems with others. It helps to discuss your worries with someone you trust. You will find a great deal of benefit in talking to persons who are caring, accepting, and non-judgmental. Such persons contribute objectivity and fair judgment, and help put our worries into proper perspective. Are things as bad as they seem? What choices do you have? The wise counsel of a minister or a committed Christian can help you see things much clearer.

But be careful from whom you take advice. Some people are well meaning, but have no spiritual interest. Godly people give godly advice. Do not expect to receive acceptable spiritual advice from just anyone.

Daniel, Shadrach, Meshach, and Abednego had each other. They prayed together, talked together, and stuck together. They provided great emotional support for each other.

Live a Balanced Life

The key to maintaining good overall health is living a balanced life. All work and no play not only makes Jack a dull boy, it can make Jack a nervous wreck. So, schedule your work realistically. List the things you need to do each day in order of importance. Don't schedule too much. It's frustrating to have more to do than you can get done. Think of and implement ways to get more done in the same amount of time. Master your time; don't let it master you. Learn to say "no." Don't get too many irons in the fire.

Also schedule time for recreation to relax your mind. Although inactivity can cause boredom, a little loafing can ease stress. This should not be a constant escape, but occasionally you deserve a break. Do something you enjoy. Plan time off for recreation. Don't leave it to chance. You'll begin to anticipate it. And above all, don't feel guilty about goofing off some of the time.

Daniel had a balanced life. He not only ran the most powerful government on the earth, he also managed to get alone at least three times every day to pray, and he allowed nothing to interfere with that. You can do the same.

Keep Looking Up

Living a balanced life includes a proper relationship with God. Remember, the Lord is an ever-present help in time of need. Someone said, "Sorrow looks back; worry looks around; faith looks up." Looking up always helps us with our stress. It helped Shadrach, Meshach, and Abednego. When they were about to be thrown into the fiery furnace, they said, "Our God whom we serve is able to deliver us from the furnace of blazing fire" (3:17). When Daniel was about to be thrown in the lions' den, the king reminded him, "May your God . . . deliver you" (6:16). Confidence in God sustained them in their hours of distress.

This confidence has always been the hope of the people of God. At times the apostle Paul could have been overwhelmed with the pressures of life, but he wasn't. Why? Because he had supreme confidence in God. He wrote,

> Do not worry about anything, but in everything by prayer and supplication with thanksgiving let your requests be made known to God. And the peace of God, which surpasses all understanding, will guard your hearts and your minds in Christ Jesus. (Phil 4:6-7)

Trust God and peace follows.

It shouldn't be surprising that Paul experienced peace in the midst of stress. Jesus promised that it would be available to everyone, including us, if we would trust God to provide it. He promised,

> Come to me, all you that are weary and are carrying heavy burdens, and I will give you rest. Take my yoke upon you, and learn from me; for I am gentle and humble in heart, and you will find rest for your souls. For my yoke is easy, and my burden is light. (Matt 11:28-30)

*   *   *   *   *

Remember, stress is a part of life, but we can learn to manage it by maintaining good physical, mental, moral, and spiritual health; seeking the support of others; and living a balanced life. . . . These are the ways to keep from being "so uptight you twang in a strong breeze."

Suffering

Are You Groping, Moping, Doping, or Hoping?

Nothing shakes our faith in God quite as much as to see unjust and senseless suffering. A young mother learns she has terminal cancer. A bus taking a church group to a ski resort overturns, injuring many and leaving one young person permanently paralyzed. A child crossing a street is struck by a car and killed.

True stories like these fill our daily newspapers. They invade our coffee time conversations. They are the substance of countless prayer requests. All around us good people are hurting.

We want to believe in a just and fair world, but time and again we see the wrong people get sick, the wrong people be hurt, the wrong people die young.

"Why, God?" we ask. Why me? Why them? Why us? Why do the worst things happen to the best people? How could a good God make a world like this, where so much of the suffering seems to fall on those who least deserve it?

We have in the Old Testament character of Job, a man who wrestles with this very question. The book of Job is probably the oldest book in the Bible. It is fitting, I think, that it grapples more earnestly with our oldest and most perplexing problem than any other book in the world.

The book of Job is a real-life drama that begins like a fairy tale. Job is one of the wealthiest, most respected, and godliest persons in the east. He is surrounded by what are commonly regarded as unmistakable tokens of divine favor: a large and loving family; immense herds of cattle, sheep, and camels; vigorous health; a good reputation; and great power. It looks as if every cloud in Job's sky has a silver lining. But before the story progresses very far, the dark clouds of tragedy begin to gather over Job's pleasant life. Before the storm is over, Job loses everything he values except his life and his faith.

He is suddenly plunged, by the misfortunes of his life, into such depths of sorrow and loss that he feels abandoned by God. Job's wife and friends add to his misery by offering him wrong advice and easy explanations for his agonizing experiences. In all of this Job's faith bends but does not break. And in the end God vindicates Job's character by restoring to him more than he had originally lost.

The story ends as it began, with Job blessed and happy. In between Job grapples with life's most common and distressing question: "Why do the worst things happen to the best people?" As we walk with Job through his gut-wrenching pain, he teaches us more how the righteous respond to the hurts of life than why those hurts actually happen.

There are five scenes in this drama. The book opens on earth with Job introduced as a highly successful, God-fearing, clean-living businessman. This is the essential premise of the book. Job is a good person who doesn't deserve what is about to happen to him.

Scene two shifts to heaven where Satan appears before God. The Lord asks Satan, "Have you considered my servant Job?" The Lord obviously reads Satan's mind and knows that he would like to destroy Job.

What do you believe about Satan? The Bible presents him as a person, not just as an evil influence. The name "Satan" means "adversary" or "opponent." So Satan is presented in Scripture as the personal enemy of both God and humanity.

Satan has set his heart on Job. He knows if he can get this good man to become bitter and doubting, he will not only have destroyed his faith, but will also cast a shadow over the credibility of God in the minds of others.

Satan can't deny that Job is a good person morally or religiously. So he calls his character into question by insinuating that the only reason Job is serving God is for what he can get out of God.

Under pressure, Satan suggests, Job's faith will melt. He is sure that a few trials will reveal a shallow and superficial faith. If he can afflict Job, he will turn from God.

You impact by the way you react.
Laurie S,

Tests are for our benefit.

The Lord knows better. No one knows the quality of one's faith until it is tested. So God grants Satan permission to test Job. The charge has been made, and God will defend the character of this good person.

Scene three shifts back to the earth where Job is suddenly crushed by overwhelming calamities. Part of his vast herds are stolen, and their attending servants killed. The remainder of his flocks are killed by a sudden lightning storm. Finally, all ten of his children are killed in a cyclone.

Suddenly Job finds himself desolate, but through it all he hangs on to the slender thread of faith. He worships God, saying, "The Lord gave, and the Lord has taken away; blessed be the name of the Lord," and in it all he "did not sin or charge God with wrongdoing" (1:20-22).

This is not the response Satan had hoped for. He had hoped that Job would become bitter against and curse God. Job is such a good man with such a far-reaching influence that if his faith in God can be shaken, the tremors will be felt everywhere he is known. Others will be watching Job, and his reaction will also affect their faith. (This is still one of Satan's favorite tactics.)

Scene four shifts back to heaven. This time Satan contends that the test of Job's faith has not been severe enough. So he asks for permission to afflict Job's body. If allowed to do so, he feels confident that Job will then curse God. Again God gambles on Job's character. Satan is granted permission to afflict Job with pain, but he is forbidden to take Job's life.

Scene five shifts to the earth again. This time Job's body is smitten by hideous sores. In excruciating pain he goes to the city dump, the place for discarded things, and sits on an ash heap in despair. His pain is made even more unbearable because he cannot understand why all of this is happening to him.

There are three very clear truths in this story. First, it is Satan—not God—who causes Job's suffering. This is one of Satan's greatest acts of deceit. He causes the sorrow of the world, but is so cunning

You impress people from afar – but you impact one on one.

that God gets the blame. God gave Job all he had. When this distressing experience is over, God will give Job twice as much as he had before. Why in heaven's name would God take it all away from him? To be sure, over every trial you experience must be written the word "permitted." God is sovereign, but God does not cause everything.

Second, these tragedies do not come to Job because he is bad, but because he is good. They do not come because he lacks faith, but to destroy his faith. If you wonder, "What has Job done to deserve this?" the answer is easy: he has done nothing. In fact, God calls Job one of the best of all persons.

Third, Job never knows about the scenes in heaven. He is left to suffer without ever knowing why. All he knows is that his wealth is gone, his children are dead, and his body is wracked with pain.

While Job sits and suffers in silence, his wife speaks to him: "Do you still persist in your integrity? Curse God, and die" (2:9). Remember, Mrs. Job has suffered, too. She has lost her family and possessions, and now her husband's health has left her faith in ruins. Her conclusion is: "Job, you have been true to God, but God has not been true to you. We can't change what is happening to us, but at least you can have the satisfaction of having the last word. Why don't you curse God and end it all?"

Fortunately, Job is wiser than his wife. While there is much he does not know, he at least knows that cursing God is not the solution to his problem. He has taken the good of life with gratefulness. Now he will accept his loss with quietness and courage. There will be no word of bitterness or despair from his lips.

Three of Job's friends come and sit with him for seven days and nights without saying a word. Job's agony is such that anything they say will be of little comfort.

In time the awesome reality of what has occurred begins to dawn on Job, and he starts to complain bitterly about his condition. At this point everything looks utterly hopeless to him. Depressed and distraught, Job wishes he could die. He wishes he had never been born. He is no longer sure even about eternity. He asks himself, "If mortals die, will they live again?" (14:14). Feeling that God has deserted him, he cries out, "Oh, that I knew where I might find him, that I might come even to his dwelling!" (23:3).

Sorrow and suffering can so shake your faith that they cause you to question almost everything you once held sacred and true. Have you ever felt that way? You may be feeling that way right now. You are hurting, and you don't understand why. You see no light at the end of the tunnel. You are saying, "Oh, God, if you are a loving God, why did you let this happen to me?"

When Job starts to complain, his friends feel compelled to explain why all this has happened. They mouth the oldest and most common explanation for suffering. While they argue from different perspectives, they all come eventually to the same conclusion. It can be summed up in the words of Eliphaz:

> Think now, who that was innocent ever perished? Or where were the upright cut off? As I have seen, those who plow iniquity and sow trouble reap the same. (4:7-8)

These friends point to the law of harvest: we reap what we sow. Job is suffering because of his sins. The judgment of God has come upon him.

Job's friends think that all suffering is sent upon people as punishment for their sins. If we are great sufferers, we have been great sinners. If our sins have been secret, then suffering is an evidence of our hypocrisy.

There is a hint of truth in what these three friends say. The law of the harvest is real. We do reap what we have sown. Judgment day is coming. We must not expect to escape the consequences of our actions forever. On the other hand, we should not expect justice immediately. If we do, we are destined to disillusionment. We all know of good people who suffer and evil people who prosper. Complete justice is never promised in the here and now, and we should not expect it until the end of time.

Job's friends make a second mistake. They try to explain to Job why he is suffering. This is the height of presumption. We may know why we are suffering in a given circumstance, but God doesn't reveal to us why someone else is suffering. God may reveal it to them, but not to us. While these friends of Job mean well, the way they proceed to deal with his crisis make an already bad situation worse.

Job is not a perfect man, and he knows it. However, his sin is not serious enough to merit all that is coming to him. After all, you don't treat dandruff with a guillotine. Job's present judgment in no way matches his sins. It is too severe for what he may have done. So Job vehemently and consistently denies their accusations.

Job's friends come to him with the best of intentions, but instead they hurt him deeply. If we are wise in trying to help our hurting friends, we will not make the same mistake. The ministry of silence is often of more value than the ministry of words. Sitting quietly with a suffering friend is often the best comfort we can give. We should take more the position of humility before sorrow and pain, realizing that there is no one sure answer and often no answer at all.

Then comes Elihu, a young intellectual. Intellectuals are people who deal in second-hand experience. Most of what they know is what they have read in a book or what someone has told them. That makes them *real* experts. Elihu emphasizes the creative value of suffering. His idea is that Job's suffering is not so much punishment for sin as it is to teach him lessons he needs to learn; it is corrective rather than punitive.

Again there is some truth in this explanation. Suffering can teach us much. God can and does use all kinds of experiences—even those God does not cause—to make us more like His son, Jesus Christ. Some testings are even designed by God to accomplish His gracious purpose in our lives.

Don't miss the fact that the arguments of these friends are not God's arguments. They are God's record of humankind's arguments, and humankind's arguments are wrong. God renders a final verdict on the arguments of Job's friends by saying to Eliphaz, "My wrath is kindled against you and against your two friends; for you have not spoken of me what is right, as my servant Job has" (42:7).

It is not until chapter 38 that God appears and speaks to Job. God comes in a whirlwind and takes Job on a mental tour of the universe. God points out the constellations in the heavens and says to Job, "Where were you when I put the stars in their orbit? Where were you when I placed the planets in the heavens?"

Then God takes Job on a tour of the animal kingdom. He points out the features of several animals and asks Job, "Can you explain why I made these animals the way I did?" In all, God asks Job sixty-five questions about creation and the government of the universe. Stumped by God's questions, Job begins to realize that humans, with their finite minds, ought not to expect to understand all the mysteries of God's working in the world. If he cannot explain the physical universe, how can he presume to question God's running of the moral universe? It is all about human capacity.

Awed to silence, Job is driven to his knees in humility at the power and wisdom of God. The frail creature bows before the mighty creator and declares, "I had heard of you by the hearing of the ear, but now my eye sees you" (42:5).

In all of this God does not answer any of the questions in Job's mind, but God does answer the need of Job's heart. God does not give Job an answer to the question, "Why do the worst things happen to the best people?" Rather, God gives Himself as the answer—His companionship, His courage, His hope. That's what Job needs, not an explanation from God, but an experience with God. And that's what he gets.

In God's presence Job's doubts melt away. Job learns that God cares about him and that he rules the world in wisdom and power. Job is now able to face his suffering without knowing why all this has happened.

This is the great message of Job: God does not owe us an explanation of life. The ultimate answer to suffering is hidden in the wisdom of an all-powerful, all-knowing, all-loving God. If we are to survive and thrive in life, we must trust God's wisdom and sovereignty. We must have the kind of faith that keeps trusting and serving God even when we do not know why bad things happen to us.

In Job's old age God restores his health and wealth, and gives him another loving family. The book of Job ends as it begins, with Job blessed and happy. His experience shows that God is able to keep the feet of saints on solid ground and that God's grace is sufficient for them. It reminds us that whatever suffering may come to us in the permissive will of God may be met by the grace of God. God's provision is sure.

The importance of the experience of Job is not that it teaches us why the righteous suffer, but that it teaches us how to cope with the hurts of life. There are four ways we can respond to the mysteries of suffering—all of them wrong except one. We can grope our way through, we can mope our way through, we can dope our way through, or we can hope our way through.

Why Me?

We can go through life asking questions, searching for answers, wanting to know, "Why me, Lord?" It is not wrong to ask "Why?" but God seldom answers us. "Why?" is not a request for information; it is a cry for help. The person who asks, "Why me, Lord?" is not wanting an answer, but rather a change of circumstances. Like Job, we most often must live in ignorance of what is going on "behind the curtains."

Woe Is Me!

Instead of asking "Why me?" we can give way to self-pity and lament, "Woe is me." Self-pity is easily the most destructive of the nonpharmaceutical narcotics. It is addictive, it gives momentary pleasure, and it separates us from others and from reality.

Don't let your feelings become the most important thing in your life. Don't brood resentfully over what happens to you. When you add self-pity to your problems, you simply compound them.

I have a longtime friend who years ago lost a leg in a work-related accident. As a result, he has spent the last thirty years walking on an artificial leg. He said to me recently, "Paul, if you ever get crippled, major on what you can do, not on what you can't do." That's the positive approach to life.

Dry Tears, Dull Joys

Another way to cope with suffering is through the use of drugs. We can take a drink, smoke a joint, or pop a pill. Taking drugs is the single most acceptable way to cope with hurt. Doctors even say at times, "Don't worry; I'll give you something." But I have learned from experience that if drugs can dry your tears, they can also dull your joys.

Even If He Kills Me

Job did not try to avoid his problems by choosing the path of drug use, but he did not take his hurts lying down. His speeches contain some of the most profound expressions of pain, despair, and outrage in all of literature. In them he wanders just to the edge of blasphemy. Though he questions God's fairness and goodness and love, and despairs of his own life, Job refuses to turn his back on God.

"Even if he kills me, I will trust in him" (13:15), he defiantly insists. He may have given up on God's justice, but he stubbornly refuses to give up on God. At the most unlikely moment of despair, he comes up with brilliant flashes of hope and faith. We, too, can cope if we have hope. How do we get hope? We find it in Jesus Christ.

* * * * *

We do not understand the problem of suffering one bit better than Job did. We come to life having nothing whatsoever to do with bringing ourselves here, and we often suffer unjustly. Why? How could a good God make a world like this? We do not know.

Even though we may not understand the problem any better than the people did in Job's day, we have more reason to be reconciled to it. For, in the meantime, God came here in the person of Jesus Christ to become a partaker with us in our suffering. The story of Jesus, the world's most righteous person and the world's greatest sufferer, is an illustration of God's suffering with creation. We ought not to have any difficulty in believing it is all for some good reason, even though we cannot now understand what it is. One day, when all has come to fruition, we shall praise God for having given us such an existence.

The Midlife Crisis

Flipped at Fifty

Dear Ann [Landers]:

I'm a 30-year-old woman with 2 preschool children, and I am 8 months pregnant. I have been married for 10 years. Our marriage was a good one. We had no major problems, and when we had problems, we always worked things out. We rarely fought and always did things together.

Last month my husband came home from a business trip and told me he was in love with another woman and is planning to leave me after the baby is born. He said his mind is made up, and he is just waiting to hear when she will be moving to this city.

According to him, he has never felt this kind of love before. He says he knows what he is giving up—a beautiful family—and is willing to pay the price. According to him, he loves us both, but the passion for her is much stronger.

My husband is 37 years old, has a good job, doesn't do drugs or drink. When I asked him to go for counseling, he said, "No one can help me. I must help myself."

My dreams of a beautiful family are shattered. I have no real friends in this state and no family. I've been busy raising my children. He does not want a divorce. He just wants to move out and live with this other woman. He says he will pay the bills until I am ready to go to work when the new baby gets a little older.

Why is he doing this, Ann? What can I do?

—Desperate in Mid-America

A midlife crisis is the time when we realize we are growing old and feel life is over. It comes when we sense we will never reach all our goals, fulfill all our dreams, or climb all our mountains. Or perhaps we have succeeded, but not found success satisfying. A midlife crisis is a time when we ask ourselves: "Who am I? Is all this worth it? What really matters in life?"

Those going through a midlife crisis look to the future and see the end of life approaching. The fact that they have twenty-five or thirty productive years left doesn't matter. Life is over. Everything is downhill. The midlife crisis is more perception than reality.

Most men reach their midlife crisis between 35 and 50 years of age. It comes about the time of the proverbial "5 B's"—baldness, bridges, bulges, bunions, and bifocals. The midlife crisis is marked by boredom—an overall unhappiness with life, job, and marriage. Life has grown stale.

There are several symptoms of midlife crisis. Depression is a symptom. Persons feel they are tied to a treadmill, trapped in a job or a marriage that is unfulfilling and unsatisfying. Another symptom is self-pity. Persons feel that life is not fair, that they "deserve more than this." Then comes fantasy, dreams of sailing away from it all. There is a desire to escape the monotony and everyday pressures of life. Persons want to find new meaning, recover lost youth, and enjoy what they feel they have missed in life. The midlife crisis is almost like entering a second childhood or adolescence.

Midlife is a time of high risk for marriages. Extramarital affairs and career disruptions are common. Some men and women seek a younger partner, someone who will make them feel alive and exhilarating. Some seek a different job. Others create a new lifestyle. Those who remain committed are still battered by a hurricane of fears, frustrations, and futility.

Sociologists, psychologists, and psychiatrists generally agree that all men go through a midlife crisis to some degree. Increasingly, this is also true of women. While our modern values and lifestyles have intensified the idea of a midlife crisis, it is not new.

In Alfred Lord Tennyson's story of Gareth and Lynette, Gareth, before he could accomplish his purpose and win the rank of knight, had to face four fierce foes: (1) the knight of the morning star, (2) the knight of the noonday sun, (3) the knight of the evening star, and (4) death. This was the poet's way of saying that youth, adulthood, and old age each bring their particular and peculiar perils and give us difficult battles.

David said the same thing long before Tennyson. In Psalm 91:5-6 he spoke of "the arrow that flies by day, or the pestilence that stalks in darkness, or the destruction that wastes at noonday." David knew from experience the perils of midlife. He was a victim of "the destruction that wastes at noonday."

David had the literary skills of Shakespeare, the musical genius of Beethoven, the athletic skills of Herschel Walker, the organizational ability of Bernard Baruch, and the military genius of George Patton.

There is more biographical data about David than any other Bible character. We learn much about his feelings and his faith by reading the Psalms. David may have been an unwanted child in an unhappy home. His father, Jesse, had been previously married and had 7 sons. His mother had been married before and had 2 daughters. David was born when these children were grown. Imagine the strife and tension of being the youngest with 7 half-brothers and 2 half-sisters.

The Lord sent Samuel to the house of Jesse in Bethlehem to show him which of Jesse's sons would be the new king. Jesse's older sons were tall, handsome, and muscular. Samuel then asked Jesse if he had any more sons. Jesse replied, "There is only one left. He is the youngest, and he's out keeping the sheep." The Hebrew word for "youngest" means the one who is least in importance. Jesse was saying, "He's not much. He's the runt of the litter." Samuel was immediately impressed that David was to be the new king. David was fourteen years old when Samuel anointed him king.

A few years later Israel was in battle with the Philistines. David went to the front with food for his brothers, who served in the army. Every day a Philistine giant named Goliath came to the edge of the valley and taunted the Israelites. He challenged them with hand-to-hand combat, called them names, and ridiculed God. Goliath, clad in full battle armor, was ten feet tall.

The Israelites were terrified. No one had the courage to accept Goliath's challenge. David, led by the Lord, volunteered to take him on. He was convinced God would give him victory over this enemy. Armed only with a slingshot, he marched into the valley to meet Goliath. (Don't be deceived by the slingshot. It was a lethal weapon. Shepherds commonly used slingshots to protect their sheep.)

David picked up five smooth stones from the brook and put them in his shepherd's pouch. When Goliath saw that David was just a boy armed with nothing but a slingshot and a shepherd's staff, he said, "Am I a dog, that you come to me with sticks?" (1 Sam 17:43). He cursed David and the God of Israel. David replied, "I come to thee in the name of the Lord of hosts, the God of the armies of Israel . . . The Lord will deliver you into my hand" (vv. 45-46). Then Goliath charged him. David launched a rock from his slingshot and hit Goliath between the eyes, his only vulnerable spot. Stunned by the hit, Goliath fell. David then rushed over, took Goliath's own sword, and killed him. Israel's army then immediately attacked and routed the Philistines. This amazing feat catapulted David into national prominence. He was an overnight hero.

At first, Saul loved David and made him one of his aids. In times of depression he would ask David to play his harp for him. The music would temporarily soothe the savage beast within Saul. But Saul became paranoid. He hated David and tried to kill him.

David was forced to flee into the desert where he lived for ten years and where he become king in Hebron. The northern tribes remained loyal to Saul, but the southern tribes were loyal to David. For seven and a half years he was king of southern Israel.

Then Saul was wounded in a battle against the Philistines. He committed suicide when it looked as if he would be taken prisoner.

At last, David became king of Israel. This was the beginning of the golden age of Israel's history. David moved his capitol to Jerusalem, built a palace there, united the twelve tribes into one nation, and drove out their enemies. Under David, Israel became the strongest nation in the Middle East. David was very successful. Firmly entrenched as king, he soon became very wealthy and powerful. He was on top of the world.

At age fifty, David fell victim to a midlife crisis. Twice in Scripture he is called "a man after God's own heart" (1 Sam 13:14; Acts 13:22). He longed to be like God in all his ways—until he had an affair with another man's wife. The story of David and Bathsheba is the best-known story of unfaithfulness found in the Bible.

David's reign led him increasingly to administrative duties. He was much too valuable to fight with the army. He spent less time in the physical kind of life and existence. His inability to sleep perhaps had a direct connection with what was happening inside of him during midlife as he was increasingly forced to assume different roles.

One night when David couldn't sleep, he went for a stroll. He looked across the way and saw Bathsheba taking a bath. What went through David's mind? A new girlfriend gave him pleasure and satisfaction when he was a teenager. Why shouldn't it happen again? After all, romance dispels monotony, emptiness, boredom, and depression. Maybe that was it. David sent for her, had sexual relations with her, and sent her home. He never intended anything more to come of it. She was married to Uriah, one of David's choice commanders. He was one of "David's Thirty"—his Green Berets. David had never lost one of these troops in battle.

Then Bathsheba sent word to David that she was pregnant. His creative mind went to work. A cover-up was needed. But how? He would have Uriah sent home, let him spend the night with his wife, and he would think the baby was his.

He ordered Uriah home. After Uriah gave his report, David suggested he spend the night at home and return the next day. Uriah's loyalty to David was so deep, he could not enjoy the comforts knowing the troops were in battle. He slept in the barracks with David's other soldiers. David was even more distressed. What would he do? He needed time to think.

David asked Uriah to stay another night. He invited him to dinner and made sure Uriah had too much to drink. The alcohol, he thought, would inflame his emotions, and he would go to his wife that night. Again Uriah spent the night in the barracks.

The next day David penned a note to Johab and sent Uriah to deliver it. It was, in effect, his own death warrant. The note read, "Put Uriah on the front lines. When the fighting is at its worst, have everyone but Uriah retreat." He would be killed, and no one would ever know.

David thought the whole affair was over, but for almost a year he was haunted by guilt. After all, he was a man after God's own heart. How could he forget it? The prophet Nathan confronted David with his sin. David readily confessed. He was relieved that the charade was over. Psalms 51 and 32 reveal David's feelings before and after his confession.

God forgave David upon his confession and repentance, but there would be many repercussions from his sin. The sword had entered into David's house, and he would never again know peace in his lifetime. The child conceived in the relationship would die. Rape, murder, and rebellion would be a part of David's own family.

The moral of David's story is this: what he achieved in his early years he jeopardized in midlife and paid for the rest of his life. What happened to David can also happen to you and me. No one is exempt from the perils of the midlife crisis, but there are several ways to avoid the "destruction that wastes at noonday."

Beware of Fantasizing

Why do people get involved in illicit affairs? Invariably, a set of circumstances sets them up. Like David, they think of the affair as a way to satisfy the discontent they feel. They begin to fantasize and daydream. The problem with fantasizing and daydreaming is that the more they are indulged, the more they prepare someone for an affair. The Bible tells us, "As a man thinks in his heart, so is he" (Prov 23:7). If we dream of sin, imagine sin, and plan sin, then all we need is the opportunity for sin. When it presents itself, we are already prepared for it.

Think of your mind as a field and your thoughts as seeds. To avoid sin, you must deal with the seeds in your heart. If neglected, the seeds become weeds.

· Never Stop Starting ·

Although fantacizing can be counterproductive, dreaming is the best defense against boredom. The poet Langston Hughes once said, "Hold fast to dreams, for if dreams die, life is a broken winged bird that cannot fly." Years may wrinkle the skin, but to give up interest wrinkles the soul.

Maintain a Balance in Life

Combining dreams and goals with a proper amount of work and play makes life interesting and productive. All work or all play makes life stale. Remember that there is an ebb and flow to life just as there is to the ocean. There must be a time for work and a time for relaxation, or else life becomes drab and boring. Even constant success is unsatisfying. As someone has said, "The trouble with the rat race is that even if you win, you are still a rat."

We must try to avoid being too busy or not being busy enough. Being too busy can place undue pressure on us, and it is possible to seek the company of another partner as a release from tension. Not having enough to do can give our mind and emotions time to run rampant, as David and Bathsheba demonstrated.

Nurture Your Marriage

A balanced life includes maintaining relationships at home. A neglected marriage is a powder keg waiting to explode. After having been married for 10, 20, or 30 years, there is a tendency to take one's mate for granted, to neglect the little things that cement a relationship such as talking, touching, thoughtfulness, tenderness, tolerating differences, spending time together, working together, playing together, laughing together. Remember, most marriages are wrecked by slow leaks, not blow-outs. Marriages may be made in heaven, but the maintenance work has to be done on earth.

Study, Pray, and Worship

A balanced life of wholesome thoughts, dreams, work, play, and proper emotions is further enhanced by a close walk with the Lord. If we experience a close communion with God through Bible study, prayer, meditation, and worship, then the spiritual strength that comes will be greater than any temptation. Furthermore, such a walk will promote high self-esteem, and the need to have others enhance it will be diminished.

* * * * *

The Lord Jesus wants to gather us unto himself for salvation, safety, and security. Even if we have failed as David failed, we can still confess and come back. It is a credit to David that when confronted with his sin, he did not blame Bathsheba, his wife, the pressures of running his kingdom, or the midlife crisis. He blamed himself.

We never make progress in our spiritual lives until we take responsibility for our actions and start calling things by their right names. David said six words that changed his life and that can change yours and mine: "I have sinned against the Lord" (2 Sam 12:13). That's the beginning of the end of the midlife crisis.

Rightouss Anger

Anger

Sleeping on a Bomb

A man bitten by a mad dog went to his doctor for tests. The examination confirmed his worst fears: he had rabies. The doctor assured him he would be okay with proper treatment and then excused himself from the examination room for a minute. When he returned, the man was frantically scribbling on a piece of paper. The doctor said, "Sir, you don't have to write your will. I told you I would give you a series of shots that will make you well." The man replied, "Doc, I'm not writing a will. I'm making a list of the people I want to bite before you give me those shots!"

A lot of people go through life with that attitude. Having been hurt by others, they never forget the wrong and long for a chance to bite back at them. To their own detriment they harbor resentment and anger.

The Bible is full of warnings and examples of the destructive power of anger. In fact, after the fall of humankind, the Bible wastes no time telling us of its destructive effects. Cain, the first mortal born into the world, was the first to discover its explosive power. He is a classic example of what uncontrolled anger can do in a person's life.

Outside the garden, life went on for Adam and Eve. Eve conceived and bore two sons, Cain and Abel. Then in a single verse the story leaps from their birth to their vocations as fully grown men. Cain was a farmer, a tiller of the soil. Abel was a rancher, a herder of sheep.

In time, Cain brought the fruit of his field as an offering to the Lord. Abel brought the "firstlings of his flock." The Lord accepted Abel's sacrifice and rejected Cain's.

The writer of Hebrews tells us that Abel brought a "more acceptable" sacrifice (11:4). While Abel brought the "firstlings" of his field, no such idea is found in Cain's offering. The obvious implication is that in contrast to Abel's best, Cain simply brought something. It wasn't that it was poor quality; it just wasn't his best. God always looks at the heart of worshipers. So it was the character of the brothers rather than their offering that made the difference.

The rejection had a devastating effect on Cain. He was downcast and angered. His wounded pride became jealousy and hatred toward his brother. The rejection was not Abel's fault.

Gently and mercifully the Lord dealt with Cain, seeking to cool his anger. God assured him that if he would genuinely repent, he, too, would be accepted. The Lord held out to him the promise of restored fellowship if he would just do right. But if not, the Lord warned, "Sin is lurking at the door" (Gen 4:7).

What a vivid picture! Anger is depicted as a ferocious beast crouching at Cain's door, ready to spring on him and devour him. He is told he must master his passions, or they will attack and destroy him like a wild beast.

From the dawn of civilization we are warned that jealousy leads to hatred and murder. Cain did not heed God's warning, and tragedy struck. His furious wrath blazed out, revealing the spirit lodged in his heart. His wounded pride produced envy and a spirit of revenge. Cain killed his brother Abel.

The Lord questioned Cain: "Where is your brother Abel?" Cain lied, saying, "I do not know; am I my brother's keeper?" (4:9). His defiant answer implied that he felt no responsibility for his brother's well-being. There was no repentance in his heart or remorse in his voice.

The Lord knew what Cain had done. The very ground that had soaked up Abel's blood cried out against Cain. With no remorse on the part of Cain, judgment was the only thing left. The Lord, therefore, pronounced a curse upon him. Cain was banished from the ground he had formerly tilled and had now polluted. He would be a "fugitive and a wanderer" in a wild world for the rest of his life (4:12). He would be driven from food-producing land to the desert wastelands. The word "fugitive" suggests the idea of staggering, stumbling uncertainly in a fruitless search for satisfaction. Though his life was spared, insecurity, restlessness, hard struggle, guilt, and fear were to be his constant companions.

Cain cried, "My punishment is greater than I can bear" (4:13). Fear gripped his heart. He imagined that wherever he went, others would try to kill him. But the Lord acted in mercy toward Cain. He put a "mark" on him so all who saw him would know who he was and what he had done. This would protect him from avengers.

So "Cain went away from the presence of the Lord" (4:16). There was no fellowship between them. Cain expressed no repentance for his sin and made no request for reconciliation to God. God did not lack mercy, but Cain lacked faith.

Cain married in the land of Nod, and there his sad story ended. There are two great lessons to be drawn from it. First, it portrays the tragic direction of fallen humanity. Cain went into exile without God and without hope in the world, afraid. Second, Cain's story portrays the destructive power of anger. It is a graphic illustration of the explosive power of anger in the human heart.

Anger is a universal phenomenon. All of us must contend with it to some degree. There are actually two kinds of anger: righteous anger and sinful anger. Righteous anger is not only inevitable, it is necessary. The absence of anger means indifference. Jesus was often angered at injustice and wrong. When the house of God was perverted, and when children were prevented from coming to him, he was angered. There was clearly a "stormy north side" to Jesus. The apostle Paul admonished, "Be angry but do not sin; do not let the sun go down on your anger" (Eph 4:26). He obviously believed a person could be angry without sinning.

When is anger sinful? First, anger is sinful when it expresses itself in bitterness and resentment. The problem is that "stewing" over people who have hurt us can actually be enjoyable. We have all tasted the luxury of indulging in hard thoughts against those who have injured us. Who among us have never known what a positive fascination it is to brood over their unkindnesses, and to imagine all sorts of ways to get even with them? It can be enjoyable and is not easy to give up. But this attitude is still sinful. That's why, to paraphrase the Apostle, we ought to "simmer down before sundown."

Second, anger is sinful when it is expressed in harmful ways. We must find unharmful ways to express our anger. I occasionally get ugly letters from people. When I do, I usually sit down and write them a nasty letter back, telling them just what I think of them. Then I lay the letter aside until the next day. Then I tear it up and throw it away and write the person a kind note. I have vented my anger, which I needed to do, without hurting anyone.

Because of the prevalence and power of anger, we need to take a close look at it and understand it so we can master it rather than be mastered by it.

Ignited by Pride

What is the source of anger? Where does it come from? In Cain's case, it did not come from Abel. He did nothing to incite Cain. He simply did what God commanded. Cain's anger, of course, did not come from God. It never does. Where, then, does anger come from? It comes from within.

We've all seen an apple with a worm hole in it. Where did the worm start? Did it start outside and work its way in, or did it start inside and work its way out? Fruit specialists tell us that the egg is laid in the blossom, and it hatches in the heart of the apple, so the worm began inside and worked its way out. Sin works this way, too. That's why Jesus said, "Out of the heart come evil intentions" (Matt 15:19). James wrote about the source of sin when he said,

> No one, when tempted, should say, "I am being tempted by God," for God cannot be tempted by evil and he himself tempts no one. But one is tempted by one's own desire, being lured and enticed by it; then, when that desire has conceived, it gives birth to sin, and that sin, when it is fully grown, gives birth to death. (1:13-15)

We blame our anger on others. We say, "He just burns me up." This is not true. No one can put fire into us; they can only draw it out. We also like to blame our anger on our circumstances. But give an angry, ill-tempered person a new mate, a new job, a new neighborhood or a new city, and he will soon be the same angry, ill-tempered person. The way we express our anger is learned behavior. The power and potential for anger is from within. Cain's anger was ignited by rejection, wounded pride, and unfounded jealousy. Anger is almost always related to a wounded ego.

The next time you are angry, look honestly at your situation. You will probably find at the root of your anger a wounded pride or an envious spirit. Angry people, ill-tempered people, impatient people, critical people are very proud people—too proud.

Waiting to Explode

Pride can lead to anger, and anger to destruction. Look at the force of anger. There is only one letter of difference in "anger" and "danger." Anger is a dangerous and destructive force. It is like a two-edged sword that can be used to injure both ourselves and others, or it can be used constructively and creatively.

If anger is not dealt with, it can and will express itself in detrimental ways. In a fit of rage Cain killed his brother. Jesus spoke of the force of anger when he said,

> You have heard that it was said to those of ancient times, "you shall not murder"; and "whoever murders shall be liable to judgment." But I say to you that if you are angry with brother or sister, you will be liable to judgment. (Matt 5:21-22)

Anger is the root; murder is the fruit. That is the force of anger.

A newspaper article several years ago told about Zinaida Bragantsova, age 74, who for 43 years had slept with a 500-pound bomb under her bed.

The story began in 1941 when Nazi troops advanced toward the Ukrainian city of Berdyansk. One night Mrs. Bragantsova was sitting by the window of her home using her sewing machine. Suddenly she heard a noise. She stood to see what was happening and was struck by a blast of wind. There was a hole in her roof, a hole in her floor, and her sewing machine was gone.

With the battle advancing on the town, she patched the roof and floor and continued living in the home throughout the war. After the war she wrote local officials to tell them there was an unexploded bomb under her house. No one believed her.

Years went by. Mrs. Bragantsova, advancing into her seventies, became something of a city legend. Then a new telephone cable was being laid in the area, and demolition experts were called in to probe for buried explosives.

Mrs. Bragantsova decided to try again to bring her buried predicament to the attention to officials. They decided to check. "Where's your bomb, Grandma?" asked the smiling army lieutenant sent to talk to Mrs. Bragantsova. "No doubt, under your bed?"

"Under my bed," Mrs. Bragantsova answered dryly. The woman's bed sat squarely over the patched spot in the floor covering the 500-pound bomb.

Local militia evacuated 2,000 people from the new apartment buildings surrounding Mrs. Bragantsova's small home. The army specialist exploded it. Mrs. Bragantsova's home was destroyed, and she received a new apartment.

It occurs to me that when people harbor anger and bitterness in their heart, it is like sleeping with a bomb. It can go off at any moment, leaving destruction and ruin behind.

Separates Us from God

While the force of anger can cause destruction, the course of anger affects us physically, socially, and spiritually. Physically, it showed on Cain's face. The Lord said, "Why has your countenance fallen?" (Gen

4:6). Anger elevates blood pressure and causes heart attacks, ulcers, and scores of other illnesses. Some physicians even believe arthritis is due to unresolved anger. Most psychologists are convinced that all depression can ultimately be traced to anger.

Socially, anger not only caused Cain to kill his brother, but it also destroyed his relationship with his family. Every day, marriages and homes are destroyed by the uncontrollable anger of an ill-tempered person.

More importantly, anger separates us from God. We simply cannot be right with God and wrong with others (1 John 3:10-15). The Scripture says, "Cain went away from the presence of the Lord" (Gen 4:16). This means there was no fellowship between them, not because God wanted it that way, but because Cain would express no repentance for his sin and made no request for reconciliation to God. God was not lacking in forgiveness, but Cain was lacking in repentance. Just as sin and anger separated Cain from God, so it will separate us from God. Anger always makes us homeless wanderers in the land of loneliness.

* * * * *

How can we deal with anger? First, we can express our anger. Like Cain, we can vent our frustrations physically or verbally on those around us. We can hurt others by what we say or do. On the other hand, we can repress our anger. We may chose to seethe on the inside or have a couple of shots of Scotch and forget it. But as John Powell suggests, "When I repress my emotions, my stomach keeps score." We all know what it is like to burn within, to have knots in our stomach from trying to repress something.

The best way to deal with anger is to confess it and ask God to redirect the patterns of our lives. We should repeat this formula as often as necessary. All sin tends to become habitual. The expression of anger in violent and unhealthy ways is no exception. Bad habits can be broken. New habits can be developed in their place. If necessary, we ask the forgiveness of people we may have hurt.

Most habits are not instantly changed. Time, determination, discipline, and divine help alter them. In fact, psychologists say it takes at least five years to change a behavior. That's a long time, but it's worth the effort.

I promise you that through Jesus Christ you can gain victory over sinful anger. Do you remember James and John, two of Jesus' twelve disciples? When they began following him, they were called "the sons of thunder." Do you know why? It was because of their stormy nature. Their sudden outbursts reminded one of a summer thunderstorm. They could cloud up and rain all over you in an instant.

By the end of the New Testament era, John was known as "the apostle of love." Christ made the difference in his life. The risen Christ can come into your life and transform you as he did John. If you are angry and ill-tempered, you don't have to stay that way. You, too, can become loving, patient, and gentle. You do not have to be mastered by your emotions—any of them. By God's grace you can be mastered by the Master and set free from sinful anger.

Ambition

By It the Angels Fell

Shakespeare had Cardinal Wolsey say to Cromwell, "I charge thee, fling away ambition: by that sin fell the angels." When Shakespeare wrote these words, was his advice scriptural? Is ambition necessarily the "last infamy of noble minds?"

There is an ambition that is noble, healthy, and essential. It leads us to be and do our best. Without it, we would be lazy and unmotivated. Without it, both we and the world would be poorer. But the ambition Shakespeare spoke of is sinful, worldly, and destructive. It centers on self and not God. It causes us to manipulate others and to be ruthless and dishonest. It will go to any length to achieve its end. When we yield to this kind of ambition, it produces jealousy and envy and a desire to crush our weaker opponents. It can cause us to be pleasant to those who benefit our purpose and indifferent or even cruel to those who don't.

Too much ambition leads to presumptuous self-promotion and disregard for others. Too little ambition results in laziness. The dilemma is how to find the balance. Many otherwise good people fail in their spiritual lives because they fail to do this.

An example of the potentially destructive effects of ambition can be seen in the life of Jacob, the Old Testament patriarch. Early in his life he was consumed by a ruthless, runaway ambition. By it he angered and alienated most of his family and brought untold sorrow to their lives. Taking advantage of his weaker brother, lying to his aged father, and manipulating his father-in-law's stock to his own advantage did not deter him. Ultimately, his desire to be somebody and to gain what he wanted almost destroyed him.

When he met God in a life-changing encounter, Jacob harnessed his ambition and became a servant of God and not of himself. With his new nature he was given a new name, Israel, meaning "the prince of God"—a name that would be given ever after to the

Grace

chosen people, the children of Israel. But let's return to the beginning of Jacob's story.

At the age of forty Isaac, Abraham's son, and his wife, Rebekah had no children. They began to pray that God would give them a child. Their prayers were more than answered. When Isaac was sixty, Rebekah conceived and gave birth to twin boys.

The first of these sons born was covered with red hair. So they named him Esau, which means "hairy." The second son was born holding the heel of the first, as if endeavoring to hold him back and secure first place for himself. They named him Jacob, which means "one who endeavors to trip up and supplant" or "one who takes by the heel." Jacob was the "go-getter" who would stop at nothing to get what he wanted. He was a first-class heel.

Jacob and Esau were very different. Jacob was aggressive; Esau was passive. Esau was a skillful hunter, a man of the field, governed by his impulses and the desires of the moment. The things of God, eternal things, did not interest him. Jacob, on the other hand, was quiet and contemplative. You could say he was the kind of kid who loved to lie around the tent reading books, working crossword puzzles, and playing computer games.

We get our first glimpse of the ruthless ambition of Jacob when he and his brother were still teenagers. Jacob had just cooked a pot of stew when Esau came in hungry from a hunting trip. He said to Jacob, "Let me eat some of that red stuff, for I am famished" (Gen 25:30).

Jacob was an opportunist. Esau had something he wanted, and he saw a way to get it. So he bargained, "I'll trade you a bowl of stew for your birthright" (25:31).

The birthright was "the right of birth." It belonged to the eldest son. It guaranteed him a more honorable position than his brother, the best of the estate, the richest land, and the covenant blessings God had promised Abraham and his descendants. The birthright could be forfeited, and it could be bartered, as in this instance.

Esau, who lived only for the moment, reasoned, "I'm about to die of hunger. What use will the birthright be to me then?" So he traded his birthright for a hot meal.

Anyone who would take advantage of his own brother like that would have to be a heel. Sinful ambition can cause a person to be an opportunist, causing him to take, to be ruthless in order to get what he wants.

Some years later the twins' father, Isaac, was an old man and nearly blind. He sensed that death was near. So he sent Esau to kill some game for his favorite meal and promised to bless him when he returned. The blessing he referred to was equivalent to a verbal will. It was so powerful that once given, it could never be taken back.

Rebekah overhead Isaac's promise, so while her husband waited for Esau to return, she schemed to deceive her husband into giving Jacob the family blessing. She had favored Jacob over Esau from the start. Jacob already had the birthright; she was determined that he should receive the oral blessing, too.

Jacob dressed in Esau's clothes and placed hairy, smelly goatskin on his hands and neck, and his mother prepared a substitute meal. Jacob's own ambition, fueled by that of his mother, led him to go to his father and pretend to be Esau.

Isaac was almost blind. The voices of the two boys were different, but he had a difficult time distinguishing between them. Isaac felt Jacob's neck and the back of his hands and thought it was Esau. He then ate the meal and gave the divine blessing to Jacob. Thus, by the most calculating stealth, Jacob stole the blessing intended for his brother.

When Esau learned that Jacob had outwitted him in securing the family blessing, he quickly went to his father. It was too late. The blessing, though obtained by deceit and fraud, had been given in irreversible legal form.

Esau's bitter disappointment quickly kindled into intense hatred, and he vowed to kill Jacob the first chance he got. Rebekah encouraged Jacob to flee for his life. Jacob left, and his mother never saw her son again.

Jacob traveled to Haran, 450 miles northeast of Canaan, where he met a beautiful, dark-eyed woman named Rachel. It was love at first sight. He desired to marry Rachel. So he agreed to serve her father seven years to gain her hand in marriage.

When the wedding day arrived, Laban, Jacob's future father-in-law, switched girls on him. When Jacob lifted the veil to kiss the bride, he discovered that it was not Rachel, but her older sister Leah. The deceiver had been deceived. Laban explained that, according to custom, the younger sister was not to marry before the older. Later Laban gave Rachel to Jacob, but in return he had to serve seven more years.

Jacob and his father-in-law then entered a partnership in sheep raising. Jacob manipulated the stock-breeding agreement in such a way that he became rich and brought Laban to the brink of bankruptcy. The business arrangement came to an end, and Jacob announced he was going back home.

Jacob had cheated his brother, deceived his father, and tricked his father-in-law. He would stop at nothing to get what he wanted.

Two decades before, Jacob had left to seek his fortune. Now he was returning home a successful person. But, Esau, the brother he had wronged, was still there. When Jacob learned that Esau was coming to meet him with 400 men, he was afraid.

When Jacob reached the river Jabbok, which was all that stood between him and the promised land, he sent his family and servants across ahead of him, but he remained behind to spend the night on the near shore alone.

That night, alone, the most important event of his life took place. Out of the deep of the night a stranger leapt. He hurled himself at Jacob, and they fell to the ground, their bodies lashing through the darkness. The strength of his attacker was more than the strength of a human. All the night through they struggled in silence. In the solitude and darkness a terrible thought came to Jacob that his real antagonist was not Esau, but God. The dream was so vivid, he seemed to himself to be engaged in an actual struggle with a living person. Just before dawn the stranger merely touched the hollow of Jacob's thigh, and in a moment Jacob was lying there crippled and helpless.

The sense we have, and that Jacob must have had, is that the whole battle was from the beginning fated to end this way. Seemingly, the stranger had simply held back, letting Jacob exert all his strength and almost win so that when he was defeated, he would know he was truly defeated; that all the shrewdness, will, and brute force he could muster could not get him what he wanted and the blessing of God on his life.

The stranger cried out to be set free before the sun rose. Jacob would not release his grip. Only now it was not a grip of violence but of need, like the grip of a drowning man. He cried, "I will not let you go, unless you bless me." (32:26). This blessing was not one he could have by the strength of his cunning or the force of his will, but a blessing he could have only as a gift.

Power, success, and wealth as the world knows them can come to those who will fight for them hard enough. But peace, love, and joy come only from God. God was the enemy whom Jacob fought by the river. God blessed Jacob in the early dawn and said, "You shall no longer be called Jacob, but Israel, for you have striven with God and with humans, and have prevailed" (32:28).

We do not understand the full meaning of this encounter, but we know that God not only touched Jacob's hip so he would thereafter walk with a limp, but he also touched his heart. Jacob would forever be a different person. This stirring experience was essentially an account of Jacob's religious transformation. Thereafter, his devotion to God was deepened.

Jacob became a person on a mission. His strong gifts were to be used no longer for unworthy ambitions and selfish purposes, but for God. His ambitions were mastered, his devotion deepened. He was at last a prince of God walking in the ways of Abraham. A sinner can become a saint, and an instrument of the devil can become a person of God.

Do we understand ambition? We must if we are to recognize it and control it. Worldly ambition expresses itself in three ways: the building of a reputation, the collecting of wealth, and the wielding of power.

To Be Something or To Do Something

My observation about politics in many countries is that its practitioners fall into two groups. The boys in politics are those individuals who want positions in order to be something. The men are those who want positions in order to do something.

—*Eric Severeid*

People jockeying with one another for prestige and position is nothing new even among Christians. The apostle John reproved an early church leader named Diotrephes who liked "to put himself first" in the church (3 John 9). Diotrephes wanted to be number one in the church. There is a Diotrephes in every office, in every factory, in every community, and in every church. Wherever there are people, you will find someone striving to be first, trying to make a name for herself.

The apostle Paul, pointing to Jesus as an example of humility, said he "did not regard equality with God" in order to be our Savior (Phil 2:6). He gave up all the rights and privileges of heaven and humbled himself so completely that he not only became a man, but he identified himself with the criminal element of society by dying on the cross. Jesus was never concerned about making a name for himself. He gladly left that to God. His concern was serving. That, said Paul, should be our attitude and disposition.

It is a sad commentary on modern-day Christianity that many who follow the one who made himself of no reputation are so concerned about building their own. They seek appointments to higher places. They long to be singled out for laudatory honors. They politic for positions of authority. They love to be called "doctor." They seem to be serving their own ego.

There is no place for self-serving in the kingdom of God. We must seek to serve our Lord in humility and even in obscurity if necessary and let God take care of our reputation. The Lord's counsel to Baruch is good counsel to us: "Do you seek great things for yourself? Do not seek them" (Jer 45:5). We are not to seek greatness. We are only to allow it to be thrust upon us if God wills.

In a world of people scrambling to set themselves above others, we must remember that God came in human form, born in a barn among animals. God taught that those who are greatest among us are servants, not rulers; that those who humble themselves will be exalted.

To Gain or To Give

In addition to seeking power and prestige, worldly ambition expresses itself in collecting wealth. There is always a gravitational pull to the earth. That's why we are admonished to set our "minds on things that are above, not on things that are on the earth" (Col 3:2). When a desire for wealth dominates someone, it destroys them. Ambition for riches isn't a legitimate goal for a Christian.

Wealth per se isn't sinful. It is the love of money that is the root of all evil. Why, then, do we want more money? Do we want it for ourselves or in order to be better stewards of the kingdom of God?

A few years ago the news was occupied with the overthrow of Ferdinand Marcos, president of the Philippines. He was vehemently despised by his own people. His tremendous wealth was salt in their wounds caused by poverty.

When he was ousted from power, indications of his wealth were uncovered. Among other things, Marcos' wife, Imelda, left behind 2,700 pairs of shoes. If Mrs. Marcos had changed her shoes three times a day, it would have taken her more than two years to exhaust her supply, assuming she did not buy any more.

Why would any woman want that many pairs of shoes? Or better still, why would people as wealthy as Marcos be so interested in money? He could have stepped down voluntarily and been able to spend his remaining years in his homeland in peace and comfort. He might even have been remembered as a hero. But because of his ambition, the last thing Marcos wanted was to take life easy. In his final days he clung to power as a baby clings to a bottle. This became his downfall.

Wealth may come. If it does, we are to receive it, enjoy it, and disburse it with gratitude. We are not to hoard it selfishly or squander it foolishly. We are to use it to build God's kingdom.

To Control or To Influence

Just as wealth can be used for the betterment of others or for personal gain, power can be used to control or influence. The world's pattern is to control people for personal gain. Christians also can experience an urge to direct others, change their thinking, and manipulate them. We, too, can nurse unworthy ambitions in our religious associations. When the tendency is to control instead of influence, it becomes an unhealthy ambition.

The apostles James and John, in selfish ambition, tried to use their doting mother to gain a preferred position for them in Christ's kingdom. They stooped to petty intrigue to exclude their ten brethren.

The other disciples had the same unworthy ambition. Why else would they have been so indignant with James and John for their suggestion? Even the Last Supper was not too sacred to be marred by this kind of selfish strife.

Jesus would have none of it. There must be no lobbying for office. "You do not know what you are asking" was the reply (Matt 20:22). And they didn't. They wanted the glory, but not the shame; the crown, but not the cross; to be masters, not servants.

To his ambitious disciples Jesus announced a new standard of greatness:

You know that among the Gentiles those whom they recognize as their rulers lord it over them, and their great ones are tyrants over them. But it is not so among you; but whoever wishes to be great must be your servant, and whoever wishes to be first among you must be slave of all. (Mark 10:42-44)

It is noteworthy that only once did Jesus say he was leaving his disciples an example, and that was when he washed their feet (John 13:15). It was an example of servanthood. And only once did any other biblical writer say that he left an example, and that example was of suffering (1 Pet 2:21).

We simply cannot be right with God and be grasping for power. The world clutches power for personal benefit. That can never be the Christian's driving force.

* * * * *

God sanctioned ambition as an entirely different scale of values. It must be pure, noble, and tinged with surrender and self-sacrifice. It is marked by humility, service, and sacrificial sharing. If your ambition is to build a reputation, collect wealth, or wield power, you may be in danger of destroying everything good and worthwhile in your life.

The answer to unhealthy and unholy ambition is to meet God as Jacob did. The whole story of Jacob is the saga of one who was being fitted for a task. After he conquered his worldly ambition, he became one of the great servants of God and humankind. It would never have happened if he had not mastered his ambition and become mastered by God.

Paranoia

Just Because You Aren't Paranoid
Doesn't Mean They Aren't Out To Get You

Out of all the hype surrounding Super Bowl XXII a statement by one sports journalist captured my attention. He referred to Joe Gibbs, coach of the Washington Redskins, as "the prince of paranoia." Technically, paranoia is a chronic psychosis characterized by delusions of persecution. In layperson's language, it is the feeling that someone is watching you, talking about you, doesn't like you, and wants to do you harm. These fears can range from mild to severe, and all of us have some of them sometimes.

Paranoia, in relationship to football coaches, is the fear that the opponent is spying on you in an effort to steal your game plan. Paranoia is okay for football coaches and Super Bowls, but it is tragic when the fear that people are watching you, don't like you, and are out to get you is brought into daily life. When it is, relationships are ruined, and life is miserable.

The real "prince of paranoia" in history was Saul, the first king of Israel. In some ways he was very big, and in others very small. In some ways he was commandingly handsome, in others decidedly ugly. All in one he was a giant and a dwarf, a hero and a renegade, a king and a slave, a prophet and a reprobate, a man God anointed and a man Satan possessed. With all his potential he stepped out of the will of God and became insecure, afraid, resentful, and paranoid, and in the end took his own life.

The elders of Israel went to Samuel saying they wanted a king. Their neighboring nations all had kings, and they wanted to be like everyone else. Besides, in time of war they would need someone to lead them in battle.

Their request distressed Samuel. God was the only king Israel was intended to have, so Samuel talked to God in prayer about the request. The Lord, knowing Israel's heart, said He would give the people of Israel a king. He assured Samuel, "They have not rejected you, but they have rejected me, from being king over them" (1 Sam 8:7). There is a lesson here for us. We can either have God's best or God's second best. We can have God's perfect will or God's permissible will.

The Lord told Samuel that God would send to him the one He had chosen as king. Saul had a striking physical superiority. He was a head taller than anyone else in Israel. He was handsome, likable, and he possessed great humility.

Never did a young person show greater promise or more kingly possibilities than Saul. Many people have outstanding opportunity but lack ability; others have outstanding ability but lack opportunity. In the case of handsome young Saul, transcendent opportunity and transcendent ability matched each other.

When Samuel told Saul that he was to be Israel's king, his humility showed. He said,

> I am only a Benjaminite, from the least of the tribes of Israel, and my family is the humblest of all the families of the tribe of Benjamin. Why then have you spoken to me in this way? (9:21)

The word "least" used by Saul means not only the smallest in size, but the most insignificant in importance.

Under instructions from God, Samuel anointed Saul privately as king. Then, according to Scripture, "the spirit of God possessed him" (10:10). In the Old Testament, the spirit of the Lord came upon special people chosen for special tasks—prophets, priests, and kings.

Later, Samuel assembled Israel and announced Saul as the new king. Again Saul's humility shone through, for when they sought him, he could not be found. He had hidden himself from the congregation. When he was found and anointed, the people shouted, "Long live the king!" (10:24).

The Ammonites attacked the small village of Jabesh-Gilead. When the men of Jabesh sought a treaty, the king of the Ammonites would agree only on the condition that every man allow his right eye to be put out. The right eye was the shooting eye. It was the eye a man aimed with when using a bow and arrow. And if he carried a shield, he held it over his left eye and looked through his right eye. Plucking out the right eye of each soldier would, in effect, render the troops useless.

The people of Jabesh asked for a seven-day truce. The king of the Ammonites, obviously not prepared for attack, granted their request. They then appealed to their new king for help. Saul quickly gathered an army of 330,000 men, marched against the Ammonites, and defeated them soundly. Jabesh-Gilead was delivered and remained forever grateful to Saul.

This newfound success went to Saul's head like new wine. He became self-willed, arrogant, and rebellious. He began to act independently of Samuel, his spiritual advisor. He became disobedient to God, and there followed a series of dismal defeats at the hands of his enemies.

The closing pages of Saul's life story are draped in black. In battle against the Philistines, his three sons were killed, and he was wounded by an arrow. Rather than fall into the hands of the enemy and be abused by them, he fell on his sword and killed himself—one of the six people in the Bible to commit suicide. When the Philistines found his body, they cut off his head, stripped him of his armor, and sent both back to their own camp to publicize the victory. They then fastened the headless body of Saul to the wall of the city and left it there for public display.

There is a tragic lesson here. The advantages and opportunities of youth never guarantee success in adulthood. One must keep true to God always. Saul was qualified in many ways to be a great leader, but his self-willed spirit prevented fulfillment of that potential.

One of the darkest experiences in the tragic life of Saul was his relationship with David. After the spirit of the Lord departed from Saul, he was given more and more to periods of deep depression. Music soothed the beast within him, so a young harpist named David was brought to the palace to play for the king. The sweet music brought momentary relief to Saul's ravaged soul.

When David killed Goliath, Saul recognized his ability and made him a commander in his army. David was loyal, capable, and devout in every way. He soon captured the hearts of Saul's servants and the citizens of the country. The people even wrote a song about his military feats. It went, "Saul has killed his thousands, and David his ten thousands" (18:7).

Increasingly, David's success and popularity bred uneasiness and distrust in the distorted mind of Saul. He feared that the charisma had already gone out of his own life. He saw David as aspiring to the throne. Apprehension mounted to jealousy, and jealousy to suspicion, and suspicion to fear, and fear to an intent to kill. Emotionally and socially insecure, Saul soon betrayed himself.

In time, Saul drove David from his palace. Then for ten years he hunted him as a wild beast in the wilderness. David loved Saul with all his heart, but Saul's paranoia destroyed the relationship.

The paranoia of Saul was a mixture of many emotions. These emotions, if left unchecked, can have the same destructive effects in any life. The experience of Saul and David in 1 Samuel 18 tells us what these emotions are and how they can destroy us.

Jealousy

Jealousy is the fear of being replaced or of loss of position or affection. When Saul heard the song the people sang about David, he became insanely jealous and said, "They have ascribed to David ten thousands, and to me they have ascribed thousands; what more can he have but the kingdom?" (18:8).

When Saul was first chosen as king of Israel, he had a poor self-image. He felt unworthy and insecure. But God gave him a new heart and made him a new person. With the spirit of the Lord upon him, his fears of failure and incompetence vanished. They were replaced by a confidence and assurance that came from God. Tragically, when the spirit of the Lord departed from him, Saul's old feelings of insecurity returned. Depression and jealousy began to surface.

Our jealousies almost invariably tell us more about ourselves, especially our self-esteem, than they tell us about others. Nothing in all the world ought to give us a better self-image, a sense of self-worth, than a right relationship with the Lord. Some people, even some Christians, have missed this. It stems in part from a misunderstanding of humility. Some people think that humility is self-depreciation. But humility is not thinking bad about oneself.

Some old hymns have even contributed to this false view of ourselves. Years ago Isaac Watts wrote a hymn entitled, "Alas, and Did My Savior Bleed." In the original words of that song the writer told of Jesus dying on the cross for "such a worm as I." In a newer version that line has been changed to "a sinner such as I." Nowhere in all of God's Word do we hear God address us as worms. Sometimes people in the Bible called themselves worms, but God always affirmed, "My son, my daughter, I love you."

We are not worms—at least God doesn't think so. God considered us valuable enough for Christ to die for us. That means we are somebody. We are something special. We are the children of God, made so by the Lord Jesus.

When Winston Churchill was a young man, he talked to a friend about the meaning of life. His thoughts were suitably philosophical and typically candid. "We are all worms," he said. Then he added, "But I do think that I am a glowworm." If we are worms, we are at least glowworms. We have been transformed, made new by the power of Jesus Christ.

A right relationship with God and thus a good self-image is one of the best defenses against jealousy that most often grows out of our own insecurity.

Suspicion

In addition to jealousy, paranoia expresses itself in suspicion (18:9). Saul was convinced that David harbored political ambitions. But there was absolutely no basis for this. It was all in Saul's mind. The

Bible makes this clear by telling us that David "had success in all his undertakings" (18:14).

To be happy and healthy, we must learn the difference between perception and reality. Unfounded suspicion almost always ends up destroying what we fear losing, what we are trying to hold onto, and making life miserable for everyone.

I once counseled a young couple who seemingly had everything going for them. The wife was beautiful and charming. The husband was handsome and successful. His responsibilities at a major state university necessitated that he do a great deal of entertaining. His wife was a great asset to him in this. Unfortunately, her husband was insanely jealous. Every time she smiled at or entered into conversation with another man, her husband became suspicious. His imagination ran wild. Though he expected her to help with his entertaining, still he suspected her and would accuse her of indiscretions. Though she was faithful, he eventually drove her away with his suspicions and false accusations.

One of the tragedies of unfounded suspicions is that they usually end up destroying what they wanted to protect, losing what they were trying to keep.

Anger

Saul's jealousy and suspicions turned into an angry rage. Twice he tried to pin David to the wall with a spear. Why did Saul have a spear in his hand while sitting in his own home? It was because he feared someone would take his life. He would have killed David if he could. Robert Louis Stevenson was right: "Jealousy is the most radical, primeval, and naked form of admiration—admiration in war paint, so to speak."

Fear

Not only was Saul jealous and suspicious of and angry at David, "Saul was afraid of David" (18:12). David was among Saul's most loyal subjects. Twice when Saul was pursuing him in the wilderness, David had the opportunity to kill him, but he steadfastly refused. Once he caught Saul asleep in a cave and cut off the end of his robe. On another occasion David took Saul's spear and water bottle and slipped away. Later, from a distance he showed these to Saul to prove he could have killed him but didn't. Still Saul refused to believe. The fear was in his mind, and seemingly nothing would change it.

* * * * *

The wondrous power of imagination is one of God's greatest gifts to humanity. Someone said, emphasizing the importance of imagination to would-be leaders, "You have to see it before you see it, or you will never see it."

There is no doubt about it: imagination is the secret to both progress and leadership. Before an architect draws a line, he first imagines the building he wants to build. Before an author writes a word, she first pictures in her mind the story she wants to develop. Such is the wondrous power of imagination.

But there is also a dark side to imagination. We can imagine things that are not true, things that do not exist, bad things, harmful things, wrong things. We can imagine that people are watching us and talking about us, and dislike us and are out to get us when they are not.

Search your own heart for a right relationship with God, and then you can rightly relate to other people. Let God give you a healthy self-image and a trusting spirit. Let God quell the anger in your soul and make you kind. Above all, allow God to calm your fears and fill you with love, for perfect love casts out fear. Without the Lord's spirit in us, like Saul, we are open to destructive emotions and feelings.

Before we leave the Saul of the Old Testament, let us look briefly at the other Saul—the Saul of the New Testament. They stand in sharp relief and contrast to one another. Here, too, is a person of uncommon personal powers and advantages, with a call from God to a vital ministry—though a ministry involving many hazards, and having none of the outward inducements King Saul's elevation had.

What a contrast these two Sauls make! With the Saul of the Old Testament, there was progressive downgrade; with the Saul of the New Testament, there was progressive upgrade. The Saul of the Old Testament lived for self; the Saul of the New Testament lived for Christ. For Saul to die was shame and gloom; for Paul to die was "gain and glory." The Saul of the Old Testament died knowing he had played the fool; the Saul of the New Testament died knowing he had fought the good fight, finished the course, and had kept the faith. The Saul of the Old Testament who lived for self threw away his crown; the Saul of the New Testament who lived for Christ gained a crown that could never be taken away. God help us to learn from these two Sauls:

> *There's just one life, twill soon be past;*
> *Only what's done for Christ will last.*

Emptiness

When Everything Is Not Enough

Three ministers were discussing the question, "When does life begin?" The Catholic priest said, "Life begins at conception." The Methodist bishop said, "No, life begins at birth." The Baptist preacher said, "No, you are both wrong. Life begins when the kids are gone and the dog dies."

I suspect all three ministers would actually agree that life begins at the foot of the cross when a person is set right with God through faith in Jesus Christ. The fact is, there is an emptiness in us that only God can satisfy. Until we know God, we start at no beginning and work to no end so far as a satisfying life is concerned.

That is the great lesson taught by the life of Solomon. Solomon had wealth, power, fame, wisdom, success, and achievement. Yet he was plagued by a sense of emptiness and meaninglessness because he left God out of his life. The book of Ecclesiastes, Solomon's spiritual autobiography, recounts the futility of finding fulfillment in these things alone. The key word in this book is "vanity." Used thirty-seven times, it means "empty," "futile," or "unsatisfying."

Solomon testifies that worldly gain can never fill the vacuum of one's life with meaning. It always leaves us empty. It is not until the conclusion of Ecclesiastes that Solomon points us to God and the importance of establishing a personal relationship with God as the only source of reality. He wrote, "All has been heard. Fear God, and keep his commandments; for this is the whole duty of everyone" (12:13).

The magnificent reign of Solomon began with all the mystery and intrigue of a modern-day coup. King David, his father, was old. He had prematurely aged because of his sin, his family problems, and the pressures of government. Two rival factions developed in his court. One was led by Adonijah, David's eldest son and the logical successor to the throne. He began by enlisting the support of Johab,

David's strong-arm general, and Abiathar, the high priest. He boldly proclaimed himself as the next king of Israel.

When Nathan the prophet heard about this conspiracy, he had other ideas. He felt that Solomon was God's choice and the most fit to succeed his father. Solomon had received his religious training from Nathan. This wise prophet loved Solomon and had given him the name of Jedidiah ("God's darling"). Nathan went to Bathsheba, Solomon's mother, and outlined his strategy to make Solomon the new king. She must go to the ailing David and persuade him to name Solomon as his successor. While she was there, Nathan arrived and served as a witness of the king's decision.

Everything went just as Nathan had planned. David named Solomon as his successor, and Nathan quickly had him anointed as the new king. It proved to be a popular choice, for when the people learned of it, they "played with pipes, and rejoiced with great joy, so that the earth shook with their noise" (1 Kgs 1:40).

Although Solomon was only nineteen years of age at the time, his life was marked by true devotion to God and genuine humility. He loved God and walked "in the statutes of his father David" (3:3).

Early in Solomon's reign the Lord appeared to the young king in a dream and offered to give him anything he desired. This was a telling offer that would demonstrate his true nature. If all possibilities are open and there are no limits, then what one chooses in such a moment is an accurate reflection of what he is on the inside and what he truly values in life. Solomon asked for wisdom, for an understanding mind, for the ability to discern between good and evil so that he might be able to govern effectively and do the job that had been laid upon him by destiny.

It pleased the Lord that Solomon did not ask anything for himself. He asked for neither long life, riches, nor vengeance over his enemies. He only wanted wisdom to be able to govern well. The Lord promised to give him not only an understanding heart, but also riches, honor, and a long life.

Solomon's wisdom was soon put to the test. One day two harlots were brought to him to settle a dispute. These two lived together, and both had delivered babies at about the same time. One night one of them rolled over on her infant and smothered him. When she realized it, she took the infant belonging to the other woman. On awakening, this one realized that the dead baby was not hers, and the two of them got into a terrible conflict over the identity of the remaining child.

When Solomon heard the case, he ordered his sword brought out and proposed to cut the living infant in half and give a half to each one of the contestants. The suggestion caught both women by surprise, and in an unguarded moment one cried, "Oh, no! Don't do that! Give her the baby rather than kill him." The other woman agreed to the proposal. Immediately Solomon pronounced the first woman the true mother and awarded her the child. The test of love had shrewdly brought the truth to light.

Under Solomon's leadership life for God's people was wonderful. The Scriptures say, "Judah and Israel were numerous as the sand by the sea; they ate and drank and were happy" (4:20). Solomon modernized and enlarged his army, and built many fortifications for the defense of the land. He inherited a kingdom that encompassed 60,000 square miles, which was ten times the territory David had inherited. Like David, Solomon shared the desire to make Israel a grand and glorious nation. Israel's splendor among the nations became a consuming passion of the newly anointed ruler.

The most remarkable construction program of Solomon's reign was the building of the temple of God. It had been in the heart of David to build a house of God. But David, because he was a man of war, was not allowed this privilege. Before he died, he gave Solomon all the supplies he had gathered for the building of the temple, including the architectural plans for its construction. So, early in his reign Solomon began building the temple of God in Jerusalem.

Cedars were cut in the forest of Lebanon, floated on barges down the coast to Joppa, and then taken overland to Jerusalem.

Stones were taken from the quarries near Jerusalem. All materials were carefully prepared beforehand so that when they were assembled, the great building was put together "without the noise of hammer." Gold, silver, bronze, and all other metals were imported.

The project took seven years to complete, and more than 200,000 workers were involved. It was a high and holy hour when King Solomon's temple was dedicated to the glory of God.

In addition to his gigantic public works program, Solomon built his empire by peaceful commerce. He controlled the trade routes south through Edom to the coast of Arabia, India, and Africa. He contracted with Hiram to build a navy and train its sailors. Its ships patrolled the seas and sailed to distant ports for precious cargo. He made Jerusalem one of the most beautiful and noble cities of the ancient world. His well-organized armies fought no wars but were able to keep the peace throughout his entire administration. Solomon's reign was a period of peace and prosperity during which Israel reached the zenith of its material splendor.

The Queen of Sheba heard of the fame of Solomon and traveled by caravan 1,200 miles from southern Arabia to learn from Solomon and to see firsthand the splendor of his kingdom. When she saw it, she said, "The half has not been told." She said concerning Solomon's subjects, "Happy are your wives! Happy are these your servants, who continually attend you and hear your wisdom!" (10:8).

It is impossible to say how much wealth came into Solomon's hands through commercial activities. We can be certain it was stupendous. He also secured vast amounts through taxes exacted from surrounding people along with the heavy burden of taxes imposed upon his own people. So wealthy was King Solomon that his soldiers had shields of gold. He sat upon a throne of ivory. And he drank and ate from vessels of gold.

There were other perks that came to Solomon. When dignitaries visited his kingdom, they brought presents of gold and silver, spices and animals. All of this added to Solomon's wealth so that "Solomon excelled all the kings of the earth in riches and in wisdom" (10:23).

The era of David and Solomon was the golden age in Hebrew history. David was a warrior; Solomon was a builder. David built a kingdom; Solomon built a temple. In the outside world this was the age of Homer, the beginning of Greek history. Egypt, Syria, and Babylon were weak. Israel was the most powerful kingdom in all the world. Jerusalem was the most magnificent city. The temple was the most splendid building on earth. Dignitaries came from the ends of the earth to hear Solomon's wisdom and to see his glory.

With honor, splendor, and power, living in almost fabled luxury, and sitting in peaceful security on the throne of David, Solomon was the one person in all the world whom others would have called happy. Yet his unceasing refrain was "Vanity, vanity, all is vanity." The book of Ecclesiastes, the product of Solomon's old age, leaves us with the distinct impression that Solomon was an empty man. He was a man who had had the best of everything—wealth, rank, honor, fame, and pleasure—but who, at the end, was disillusioned. He had everything, but it was not enough. He still felt empty and unfulfilled. In his last days he concluded that a person's chief end was to "fear God and keep his commandments" (12:13).

We are too big for this world. We can never find satisfaction and happiness in things of our world alone. We must have God. The life of Solomon is a dramatic demonstration that there is a vacuum in us that only God can fill.

Solomon made a good beginning but came to a tragic end. His great sin was the loss of devotion to God. Solomon's grand design was clouded by a grand mistake: his marriages to idolatrous women. Many of these women were daughters of heathen princes and kings, wedded for the sake of political alliances. For them, he who had built the temple of God also built alongside of it heathen altars. Thus the idolatry that David had been so zealous to suppress was reestablished in the palace. This brought to a close the glorious era ushered in by David and started the nation on the road to ruin. It began the sunset of Israel's golden age. The apostasy of Solomon's old age is one of the most pitiful spectacles of the Bible. Perhaps the account of it was intended by God as an example of what luxury and cease-less rounds of pleasure will do even to the best of people.

Solomon's life teaches us about four things that cannot fill the emptiness of the soul.

Education

At the outset of his reign Solomon was granted one wish from God. His sole request was for wisdom. It was granted, and he became the wisest man who ever lived. He wrote 3,000 proverbs; 1,005 songs; and three books of the Bible: Proverbs, the Song of Solomon, and Ecclesiastes. He knew biology, psychology, zoology, botany, and astronomy. He knew the habitats of the birds of the air, the beasts of the field, and the fish of the sea. But nothing satisfied the empti-ness in his soul. He said concerning his wisdom, "Vanity of vanities. All is vanity."

God expects us to study, learn, and sharpen our skills to their maximum. But while education can fill the mind, it cannot fill the soul.

Pleasure

Just as education cannot fill the emptiness of the soul, neither can pleasure. Solomon became a typical Oriental potentate. He indulged every desire, pampered every whim, fed every appetite. Wine, women, and wealth were his in excess. He had 700 wives, 300 mis-tresses, and everything else that went with that kind of life. But inwardly he was a miserable person.

Recently I talked with a friend who had known better days with the Lord. He had once walked in fellowship with God, but had gone away. I asked him, "Are you happy?" He responded, "No. Of course not!" He said it as if to imply, "You know the answer to that. There is no need to ask."

When I see on the marquee of nightclubs, "Happy hour, 5-6 P.M.," I think to myself, "If the owners were honest, the sign would read, 'Unhappy hour, 5-6 P.M.' " The people who frequent night clubs are not happy. They are lonely and empty. They are there because they do not want to go home. They are bored and lonely. All they will find is a momentary sedative to dull the ache in their heart. They will never find there what will fill the emptiness of their soul.

Many people caught in the fast lane of life share the disillusionment of Bonnie in the movie, *Bonnie and Clyde*. Bonnie enjoyed her life of crime at first. But she expressed the futility of it when she said, "I thought we were going somewhere, but we are just going." Pleasure is a dead-end street. Life without God leads to nowhere.

Wealth

A certain advertisement promises, "The _____ gives you the one thing you have always wanted in a luxury car—everything!" That's what Solomon had—everything! He was educated, indulged in pleasure, and was wealthy besides. But it was not enough. His reign was marked by splendor without surrender. But still he was not happy. He said concerning his wealth, "Vanity of vanities. All is vanity" (2:4-26).

I have been poor, and I am now relatively well off. Given my choice, I'll take things the way they are now. All things being equal, I'd rather have money than not have it. I keep it in proper perspective, however. I am really no happier than I was when I was working as a college janitor for seventy-five cents an hour. I understand that things will not satisfy the deep longings of my heart.

Once I stayed in the presidential suite of the finest hotel in Fort Worth, Texas. It was provided to me on a complimentary basis because it was the headquarters of the convention over which I presided. Ordinarily it costs $1,000 a night. It was quite a place for a country preacher who grew up sleeping on a pallet under the kitchen table in a small apartment. The pressures of the convention, as fine as my suite was, kept me from sleeping well. Whether you are in a $1,000-a-night suite or a second-rate motel, it makes little difference in how well you sleep.

Money will buy a bed, but not sleep; books, but not brains; food, but not appetite; finery, but not beauty; a house, but not a home; medicine, but not health; luxury, but not culture; amusement, but not happiness; religion, but not salvation; a passport to anywhere, but not heaven.

Achievement

Solomon said, "I worked hard." As a result, he enjoyed the world's standard of wisdom, pleasure, wealth, and achievement. However, none of these could fill the emptiness within him. If you give yourself to those things, you will die inside long before you are buried. As the unknown poet wrote:

> *Some men die by shrapnel,*
> *And some go down in flames.*
> *But most men perish inch by inch,*
> *Who play at little games.*

Your career, your job, your profession, your business are little games compared to eternity. Success and achievement in them can never fill the emptiness inside.

* * * * *

Be careful what you make the center of your life. Nothing in this world is big enough to fill the void except God. Life without God is like a tire out of balance.

The Bible declares that life is too important to build around anyone or anything less than Jesus Christ. John wrote, "In him was life, and that life was the light of all people" (John 1:4). Jesus said, "I have come to give you abundant life."

Some people are diligently, desperately, and frantically looking for the meaning of life, but they are looking for it in the wrong place. That was Solomon's mistake.

Passiveness

Off the Floor and Through the Door of Life

Some people have to be pushed to get them to do anything in life. They lack the initiative, the drive, the get-up-and-go to get anything done. Their motto seems to be: "Don't muddy the waters." "Let sleeping dogs lie." "If it ain't broke, don't fix it." These people are passive, complacent, and sedentary. If progress depended on them, the wheels of the world would soon grind to a screeching halt.

Isaac, the Old Testament patriarch, was much like that. He is often mentioned in the same breath as Abraham and Jacob. The Lord is often identified as "the God of Abraham, Isaac, and Jacob." Abraham, Isaac's father, and Jacob, Isaac's son, were both movers and shakers. They were people of action, initiative, and ambition. But Isaac was of a different temperament.

Abraham was a person of great faith. Early in his life he heard the call of God to leave his home in Ur of the Chaldees to go to the land of Canaan. God promised to multiply his seed as the sands of the sea, to make a great nation from him and through him to bless the whole world. Daring to believe God, Abraham acted. He left family, friends, and familiar surroundings to obey the Lord.

Jacob was a man who burned with ambition. He let nothing and no one keep him from getting what he wanted. Deceit and manipulation were the tools of his trade.

Sandwiched in between Abraham and Jacob was Isaac, who never did anything significant that we know of. All that is said of him is that he lived, had two children, and was a well-digger.

We get our first glimpse of Isaac's passive personality as a grown man. At age 40 he was still a bachelor. His father was worried. Abraham and Sarah had traveled from their home to Canaan on the strength of God's promise to make a great nation out of them. For years they had waited and prayed for an heir. Finally, when

Abraham was 100 and Sarah was 90, they were told they would have a child.

Nine months later their son was born. When this son of promise turned 40 and was unmarried, it seemed that God's original promise to Abraham may not be fulfilled. Isaac seemingly lacked the initiative even to find a wife for himself, so Abraham instructed one of his servants to find a wife for Isaac. Isaac seemed content to let Abraham take the initiative for him, an important point here.

There is no indication that anyone picked Abraham's wife for him. He chose Sarah for himself. When she died, Abraham, at the age of 140, married again and had six sons by his new wife. No one picked wives for Isaac's two sons. Esau chose a wife from among the Hittites, a decision that grieved his parents. They wanted him to marry one of his own kind. And Jacob traveled 450 miles to Haran to find his wife, Rachel. While they chose their own wives, Isaac seemingly let other people make this decision for him.

Isaac did devote some time to digging, or redigging old wells, but when neighboring tribes challenged him saying the water belonged to them, he quietly moved on to another place and dug another well. He would then be challenged again and move on again. People always seemed to shove him around and take advantage of him.

Isaac seemed to favor his son Esau, while his wife Rebekah favored the other son Jacob. That was probably because Esau was more like his father, passive in nature, and Jacob was more like his mother. When Isaac was an old man, he was deceived by Jacob and Rebekah. They both took advantage of his age and poor eyesight, but he did nothing about it. He just shrugged it off. He let it go. That was his way. Why?

Psychologists tell us that behavior is determined by heredity plus individuality. Recent studies by the University of Texas indicate that 25 percent of behavior is determined by heredity and 75 percent by environment. So what was there about Isaac's environment that made him like he was?

For one thing, he was an only child. In all probability he was pampered and coddled and missed the development that comes through sibling rivalry. He was also the son of older parents. Remember, his father was 100 years old, and his mother 90 when he was born. Finally, his family was very affluent. His father was one of the richest men of his day. He left all his wealth to Isaac. While poverty is not to be desired, it can give aggressiveness to one's personality.

Andrew Carnegie was fond of saying, "It's three generations from shirt sleeves to shirt sleeves." What he meant was that children of rich parents have a hard time finding the moral equivalent of the struggles through which their parents obtained their wealth. We are not born to be satisfied. Boredom leads to self-destruction. Struggles make us stronger. Look at the lives of the early pioneers who faced harsh climates, sparse land, and endless toil. Out of their efforts came a sturdy civilization and a sturdy people.

So, put it all together—the only son of older, affluent parents—and an Isaac can result. But circumstances don't absolve anyone of personal responsibility. We always have a choice in what we are and how we are. By God's grace we can change.

If people manipulate you, take advantage of you, and shove you around; if you lack the drive or determination to get things done; if people walk on you and make decisions for you, and you don't like it, you can change. You can take control of your life and become more assertive.

Experience teaches us there are two ways to fail in life. We can fail by trying to do something and not succeeding, or we can fail by doing nothing. Isaac, because he was so passive, seemingly wasted a lifetime of opportunity and potential because he chose the latter of these two approaches to life. Rather than taking control of his life and becoming all he could be, he chose to go with the flow and bend with the breeze. He chose to go along to get along.

What do we have to do to take control of our lives, to be more dynamic and assertive? How can we get some drive so as to reach our highest potential for God?

Not from the life of Isaac, but from life itself and from the Scriptures in general we learn the answer. There are four things we need to be successful, to move with a sense of purpose and destiny.

Direction

First, we need direction. We need clearly defined goals. We need to know where we are going.

Alice in Wonderland has a message for all of us. Alice lost her direction and did not know which way to go. She was bewildered and confused. Then she met the Cheshire Cat, of whom she asked, "Which way ought I to go from here?" The cat responded, "That depends on where you want to get to." Alice responded, "I really don't care where I get to." The Cheshire Cat wisely responded, "Then it really doesn't make much difference which way you go." Katherine Ann Porter, in her book *Ship of Fools*, said,

> I'm appalled at the aimlessness of most people's lives today; 50 percent don't pay any attention to where they are going; 40 percent are undecided and will go in any direction; only 10 percent know what they want, and even all of them don't go toward it.

Where are you going in life? What are your goals? Do you have a sense of direction? I think perhaps the most important question for every one of us is this: "When you get where you are going, where will you be?" Everyone is going somewhere—up, down, backward, or in circles. No one is standing still. If you don't know where you are going, how will you know when you get there?

A man said to his friend, "If you don't change your direction, you are going to end up where you are headed." I think that can be safely said of each of us. Fortunately, we have choices. We can change directions. We do choose where we are going in life. Those people who know where they are going are most likely to get there.

Neil Armstrong grew up in a little Ohio town called Wapakoneta. He is remembered in in his hometown as a youth who "fulfilled all the ideals of what you would expect of a typical American boy." He was especially good in science and mathematics. One night in the spring of his senior year in high school he stopped by to see his physics and chemistry teacher, Mr. Crites. He sat on the front porch, talking with Mr. and Mrs. Crites. When time came for Neil to leave, they stepped down from the porch into the light of a great silvery moon bathing the earth. Mr. Crites said, "Neil, you are a good boy. Tell me, what are you going to do with your life?" Neil smiled and looked up at the moon, "Mr. Crites, someday I'd like to visit that man up there." The teacher and his wife smiled indulgently, thinking, "Poor Neil." That was in 1946, when no one had any thought of going to the moon. But on July 20, 1969, Neil Armstrong became the first man to walk on the moon.

Dreams have a way of coming true. If you want to get off dead center, if you want to get your life moving, start with a dream. Decide where you want to go. Get some direction in your life.

Daring

In addition to direction, we need daring. Be willing to risk. Seek the courage to try. Get up and get moving. The president of a successful company was asked what it took to get to the top. "The same thing it took to get started," he replied, "a sense of urgency about getting things done."

In *The Big Switch*, her book on career changes, author Rochelle Jones stresses: "If you can dream it, begin. If you can imagine it, proceed. Commitment and vision form a momentum of their own, which brings about a successful conclusion." The people who make things move in this world and in their own lives share a sense of urgency.

No matter how intelligent or able you may be, if you don't have a sense of urgency, now is the time to start developing it. The world is full of competent people who honestly intend to do things tomorrow, or when they can get around to them. Their accomplishments, however, seldom match those of less talented people who are blessed with a sense of the importance of getting started now.

Henry J. Kaiser, one of America's greatest industrialists, said, "There is only one time to do anything, and that is today." Once when Henry was about to promise more than one of his aids thought possible, the man tugged on Henry's arm and whispered, "Take it easy, H. J. Remember, Rome wasn't built in a day." "I wouldn't know about that," Henry grunted. "I wasn't working on that job."

Motivation does not come first—action does! We have to prime the pump. If we wait until we are "in the mood," we may wait forever. When we don't feel like doing something, we tend to put it off, but it is often after we get involved in a task that we become highly motivated.

Dedication

God gave us two ends
One to think with, and one to sit with.
All the failure or success in life
Depends on which end you use.
Heads, you win;
Tails, you lose.

—plaque, University of Pennsylvania

"The Ladder of St. Augustine"
The heights by great men reached and kept
Were not attained by sudden flight
But they, while their companions slept
Were toiling upward in the night.

—Henry Wadsworth Longfellow

There is simply no substitute for hard work. Direction and daring can be rendered ineffective without dedication to a task. Hard work will make up for almost any deficiency. One of our problems is that too many people lack a commitment to work. If you go to work as late as you can, leave as early as you can, make as much as you can, and then sit on your can, you ought to get canned. And I say that candidly!

Determination

We are most active in meeting our potential when we have clearly defined goals, take risks, and stay committed to the task. Add to direction, daring, and dedication another important ingredient: determination.

A few years ago I received a long distance telephone call from a man in Vancouver, British Columbia, Canada. He told me he had recently lost his best friend in an accident. In his sorrow someone had given him a copy of one of my books, *Why Me Lord?* He was calling to thank me for writing it. He said he had not been a Christian until he read that book. Now he trusted Christ as Savior and had hopes of seeing his dear friend again in heaven.

As I hung up the phone, I reflected on the hours and hours of toil that went into that book. In fact, I reflected on my whole writing career up until that time. I had written two books earlier, and they had been approved quickly and without question. I thought I must be an accomplished writer. So I started writing a book on suffering and death, with every confidence that it, too, would be quickly published. When I submitted it to the publisher, it was rejected. I submitted it to another, and it was rejected again. Six publishers in a row rejected it. By that time I was feeling rejected myself.

I was ready to give up. I had decided that I was not a writer after all. And then I sent it to one more publisher, and the editors liked it. They changed the title, had me write several new chapters, and then published it. Today that book has sold more than any of the other thirty books I have written, and it has been printed in five languages —English, Chinese, Swedish, Indonesian, and Braille.

Persistence does pay off. If your work is rejected, it doesn't mean that you are rejected. If your work is rejected, it does not necessarily mean it is no good. The judgment of others may not be good.

Winston Churchill, Prime Minister of England during the crucial days of World War II, perhaps more than any other person helped to save the free world from Nazi domination. He was once invited to speak at the Boy's School at Harrow, his old alma mater. The headmaster had told the boys that Churchill was coming and would give an immortal message. "Bring your notebooks," he told the boys, "and copy down everything he says. You will want to pass it along to your children and your grandchildren because you are going to hear the greatest living Englishman."

The day came, and Churchill arrived. He was well along in years. He stood on the platform and put his finger in his vest pockets as was his custom, and then pulled his glasses down on his nose as he often did and looked the group over. As he stood there looking at the rough wooden benches in which initials had been carved for 600 years, his own carved among them, he no doubt saw in memory a little boy who had sat there many years before—a shy, skinny little kid named Winston Churchill—who stuttered but who became the greatest master of English speech in modern history.

He noticed how bright the students looked, but realized that life could bring them plenty of hard knocks and troubles. So he made his speech. "Never give in, never give in, never, never, never, never, never, never!" and he sat down. It was an immortal speech that they would remember until the end of their days.

You can overcome all conditions through the power given to you by Christ. Of course, there is a limit even to persistence. If at first you don't succeed, try, try again. Then give up. There's no use being a fool about it.

* * * * *

If you have lived a passive life like Isaac, and you don't like yourself for it; if you have been manipulated and used by others, and you would like to change, with God's help you can. No one has to stay the way they are.

An unknown poet spoke of the good news of beginning again when he wrote:

I played with blocks when I was a child
Houses I built and castles I piled
Till they tottered and fell, all efforts in vain
But my father said kindly, come try it again.

I played with my time. What's time to a lad?
Why pore over books, play, play and be glad.
Till my time was all spent and like the sweet summer's rain.
But my father said kindly, come try it again.

I played with my soul, my soul that is I
The best that is me, I smothered its cry.
I lulled it and dulled it and now O God, the pain!
But my Jesus said kindly, come try it again.

Commit your life to God and God's purposes, and it can become dynamic, purposeful, and happy.

Lust

The High Cost of Low Living

Sooner or later almost every person struggles with sexual temptation. Very few escape this battleground without a skirmish or two. Those who hope to be successful in the Christian life must come to grips with their sexuality and master their desires. Otherwise, ruin in the Christian walk is certain.

Samson was one of God's servants who fell victim to his own lusts and carnality. His tragic fate reminds us of what might happen to us.

Samson was endowed with superhuman strength. He was the Hercules, the Atlas, the Rambo, the Arnold Schwarzenegger of the Old Testament. Stories of his dramatic life never seem to lose their popularity.

While Samson had great strength, he also had a great weakness. Against men he was undefeatable, but in the hands of women he was as weak as water.

From his birth he was called to be a Nazarite, one consecrated to God. Instead he lived a self-willed, undisciplined, and promiscuous life. In the end he blew it all—his opportunity, his ministry, and his testimony.

What happened to Samson can happen to any of us today. Unless we bridle our desires, we could come to the same kind of disgrace, humiliation, and destruction as he did.

Samson's story, as told in the book of Judges, opens with Israel being troubled by the Philistines. This harassment had gone on for forty years. When Israel settled the promised land, there were inhabitants already there. While the Lord gave the Israelites the land, they still had to drive these people out—which was not an easy task.

The Philistines were among those inhabitants and one of Israel's most formidable foes. They were a well-organized group composed of five cooperating city-states, each under the leadership of a single ruler. Their people were good soldiers, and their weapons were the finest because they had a monopoly on iron manufacturing.

Israel found itself in need of a leader who could unite the people in resisting the growing Philistine menace. Samson was to be God's leader for this crucial hour.

The Hebrew name Samson means "sunshine." So this lad may well have gone through life being called "Sunny Boy." The Scripture makes a great leap from Samson's birth to his manhood. When next we see him, he has gone to the Philistine city of Timnath, located about three miles southwest of his home. There he met a Philistine woman whom he decided he wanted to marry.

In those days parents arranged marriages for their children. So Samson asked his parents to contact this woman for marriage. This disturbed his parents. They wanted him to marry one of his own people. They felt that taking a wife from the uncircumcised Philistines was asking for trouble. Samson's self-will was already evident. He was inflexible and emphatic. He insisted that he wanted to marry the young woman of his choice.

So Samson and his reluctant parents went to Timnath to negotiate the marriage. During the less-than-two-hour journey Samson turned aside at a vineyard, perhaps to get some grapes. While there he was attacked by a lion. In this encounter we get our first glimpse of Samson's superhuman strength. The spirit of the Lord came upon him, and he tore the lion apart with only his hands. Once in Timnath, his parents concluded the marriage negotiations and returned home.

When the arrangements were ready, Samson and his parents went back to Timnath for the wedding festival. Samson turned aside near the vineyard to see what had happened to the young lion he had slain.

To his surprise, he found the carcass full of honey. Bees will not approach a putrid carcass. But the hot dry climate had dried the dead body in a very short time, leaving a suitable cavity for the bees. They had hived there and left a fresh supply of honey. Samson scraped it out into his hands and shared it with his parents. They then proceeded to Timnath for the wedding.

The wedding feast took place in the home of the bride, and all the guests, even his best man, were Philistines. On the first day of the seven-day feast Samson challenged his thirty festival companions to a contest of wits. He proposed a riddle and a wager. Riddles were a popular form of entertainment in those days. Samson's riddle was this: "Out of the eater came something to eat. Out of the strong came something sweet" (14:14).

Samson limited the time for solving the riddle to the week of wedding festivities. As a wager, he offered to provide each man a new suit of clothes if he could solve the riddle. If the men failed, they were each to give him the same. The challenge was accepted by his thirty Philistine companions, but without the clue of the slain lion and the swarm of bees, the guests would never be able to solve the riddle.

The riddle stumped the Philistines, and the wager gravely concerned them. Accordingly, on the fourth day of the feast they threatened Samson's wife if she did not divulge the answer. She begged Samson to give her the secret. Samson succumbed to her tears and told her the solution on the seventh day. Immediately she communicated the answer to her countrymen. Provided with this information, the Philistines delivered their answer to the riddle on the seventh day.

Samson was livid. He said, "If you had not used my wife to deceive me, you would never have solved the puzzle." In anger he stormed out of the wedding feast and off to Ashkelon, twenty-two miles away, where he slew thirty Philistines. Stripping from them their clothing, he returned to pay his wager.

Disillusioned with his new wife, he returned home in hot anger, with intentions of never going back. At least this was how his father-in-law interpreted the situation, and so he gave his daughter to Samson's best man in marriage.

When he cooled off, Samson had second thoughts about his actions and returned to possess his intended bride. He even took a gift to appease her for leaving so abruptly at the time of the wedding.

When he returned, he learned that she had married his best man. The father sought to appease his hot-tempered son-in-law by offering his younger and fairer daughter as a wife. A feud then ensued between Samson and the Philistine family.

To retaliate, Samson captured 300 foxes, tied their tails together, and fastened a slow fire brand between each pair. The brands lighted, and the foxes started racing down the hillside into the corn-fields. Nothing could stop them as they ran wildly here and there through the Philistines' grain. The result was total destruction of the fields and olive orchards. The Philistines placed the blame for the outrage on Samson's wife and her family and retaliated by burning them to death.

Samson was really mad. He then attacked the Philistines with a devastating effect. Now considered a full-fledged outlaw with a price on his head, Samson fled into the Judean highlands for safety. The Philistines pursued and made a punitive raid on a Judean village. It was an act of war and could develop into a general conflict that would be fought to the greatest danger for Israel.

Samson was a Danite, so the men of the tribe of Judah felt no obligation to protect him. They rallied a posse and went after Samson themselves. Perhaps if they captured him, their Philistine overlords would be merciful to them. The people of Judah were obviously well content with the Philistine domination and resented the disturbance caused by Samson's feud with them.

When they found Samson, he did not resist their purpose to deliver him to the Philistines, but asked them to swear they would not personally attack him so he would not have to shed Jewish blood. When they agreed, he surrendered peacefully.

The Philistines rejoiced at the sight of their assailant being brought to them in fetters, but their joy was short-lived. While they were shouting in triumph, he broke the cords that bound him as though they were a string, and then he turned on them. Grabbing the first weapon at hand, the jawbone of an ass, he attacked his enemy and killed 1,000 of them.

From there Samson traveled to Gaza, the southernmost Philistine city, where we are told in unabashed frankness of his night visit with a resident prostitute. When news of his presence reached the authorities, they devised what seemed to be a foolproof plan for capturing him. They did not attempt to search the city by night, but rather locked the city gates and waited until morning to kill him. When the gates of the city were closed at night, they relaxed, believing Samson could not escape. They would move in on him at the first light of morning.

Samson anticipated their strategy and rose up at midnight. With his enormous strength he lifted the gates of the city with their posts and the bar that fastened them, and carried them to Hebron, a distance of thirty-eight miles, mostly uphill.

One would have thought that two disastrous affairs with Philistine women would have taught Samson a lesson, but no—the undaunted Samson soon had an eye for a woman named Delilah in the valley of Sorek. She was no ordinary woman. Beautiful yet calculating, a master of feminine wiles, she became Samson's downfall.

When the Philistine authorities learned of Samson's affair with Delilah, they saw this as their opportunity to conquer him. The five lords of the Philistines offered to pay Delilah 1,100 pieces of silver each—5,500 in all—if she would find out the secret of his strength.

Relentlessly pursuing her prey by insisting that if he really loved her he would not be reluctant to divulge his secret, Delilah finally extracted the deep secret from Samson. His strength lay in the fact that his hair had never been cut.

The temptress knew her victim only too well. She knew that he had told her the truth. With Samson asleep on her lap, probably in a drunken stupor, she cut off his hair. This was the only remaining part of the Nazarite vow he had not broken. Now he had violated it.

Delilah then cried out, "The Philistines are upon you" (16:20). He arose and shook himself, but the Israelite strongman was powerless before his enemies.

Samson's strength was, of course, not in his hair but in his consecration to God. His hair was only an outward sign of that consecration. When he lost his consecration, he lost his power. When Delilah cut his hair, in a sense she cut him off from God.

The Philistines seized him, gouged out his eyes, bound him with bronze fetters, and sent him to grind in the mill in the prison house in Gaza. He was reduced to humiliating slave labor.

The five lords of the Philistines decided to hold a national festival to honor their god Dagon and to rejoice that he had given their arch enemy into their hands. In the midst of the merriment they ordered Samson brought to the temple so they could gloat over his humbled condition. After they had made sport of him, he requested of the youth who was guiding him that he be led to the pillars that held up the temple roof so he could lean upon them. The five Philistine lords and a multitude of other men and women were in the temple, while 3,000 others gathered on the roof to catch a glimpse of the strongman.

In place between the pillars Samson prayed, "Oh, Lord God, remember me, I pray. Strengthen me, just this once, that I may be avenged of the Philistines for my two eyes."

Then summoning the last ounce of his strength, he pushed on the two middle supporting pillars until they gave way, and the roof of the temple came crashing down. This brought about the death of the Philistine lords and many of the spectators.

Samson stands in the Scriptures as an example of the high cost of low living. He could not be conquered from without, but he lost the battle within. He had great physical strength, but great moral weakness. The man who was able to slay a lion with his bare hands was as weak as a lamb in the hands of women.

By his sin he gave the enemies of God an occasion to blaspheme the name of God. It is true in every generation. When those devoted to Christ sin willfully, the blasphemy of evil persons against the cause of Christ is the inevitable result.

What happened to Samson can happen to us. He was not the first nor the last man of God with unusual ability to lose his opportunity, his ministry, and his testimony. He blew it all by illicit sexual involvement.

The Bible does not, of course, teach that sex itself is sin. Far from it; it is a gift from God. It was God who created us male and female. It was God who planted in us the physical magnetism between the sexes. But the God who gave us sex also gave us laws governing it. The Bible teaching is clear: it is sex under the seal and shield of marriage or total abstinence. It is chastity before marriage and fidelity in marriage. Anything else violates God's will.

Many Christians fall into extramarital affairs when they are not looking for them. They become vulnerable because they fail to realize that the romantic spark never dies inside us. They are careless in their relationships, and slip into sin before they know it and without intending it. It may be with another employee, or a neighbor, or a counselee. Two people begin to talk, to confide in one another. One of them is often divorced or in an unhappy marriage. The other listens intently and seems to care.

In the beginning the friendship is innocent, harmless, and even helpful. In time, the two begin to share intimate feelings. The light turns amber. Before long, "innocent" touching begins to take place. At first it is a social embrace, a warm pat, a friendly nudge. Both will insist there's nothing wrong with that. It is not related to sex. They are good friends and no more, or so they tell themselves. Each, however, soon becomes aware of the other's genuine admiration and acceptance. The light is turning from amber to red.

They begin spending more time together. It feels good just to be around one another. Then they realize they have much more than a casual friendship. They did not intend it or plan it. It happened because they did not take the proper precautions.

What is the bottom line in winning over sexual temptation? Following are some guidelines.

Thought Control

As with all sin, the place to control sexual temptation is in the mind. Paul's command, "Whatever is . . . pure . . . think about these things" (Phil 4:8), is the key. Jesus warned us about wrong thinking when he said,

> You have heard that it was said, "You shall not commit adultery." But I say to you that everyone who looks at a woman with lust has already committed adultery with her in his heart. (Matt 5:28)

If a person looks at someone of the opposite sex with the intent of sinning sexually, that person is lusting. If someone thinks, "I would go to bed with him/her if I could get away with it," then the purpose of that person's heart is immorality.

Your eyes are the doorways to your mind, so if you want to avoid lust, you must watch your eyes. Job said, "I have made a covenant with my eyes; then could I look upon a virgin?" (Job 31:1).

To resist lustful thoughts when talking or counseling with a person of the opposite sex, look at the person's eyes as you talk. This practice shows real warmth of the best kind. It is healthy, normal, and respectful. But a word of caution. We sometimes send signals with our eyes. Don't lock eyes with a person you are not talking to. For many, this can be a signal of sexual interest.

Tongue Control

In winning the battle with sexual temptation, thought control is only the first line of defense. Tongue control comes next. Be careful to avoid tender, intimate talk with a person of the opposite sex. Talk about real feelings and often about marriage problems, the sharing of intimate thoughts, is often the beginning of danger.

Touch Control

Thought control and tongue control are next to impossible without touch control. In families, healthy touching has its benefits; but in casual relationships, without careful controls, it can lead to disaster.

What are the guidelines for Christians? For the married, simply do not touch someone of the opposite sex. Even a touch given to someone as a mere social gesture can lead to inner pleasure for the other person.

* * * * *

Even if you have failed in the intimate area of your life, I have good news for you. The God of Samson is the God of the second chance. In his blind and miserable condition Samson prayed for strength, "Just once more," and God heard him. God will do that for you and for me.

Shining through the Bible is God's readiness to forgive sin, sexual or otherwise, and God's eagerness to bring peace of mind and heart to the repentant. Concerning sexual sins Jesus always dealt tenderly. There is no more wonderful illustration of Christ's compassion than his defense of the woman taken in adultery.

Ringed by the self-righteous ones about to stone her, he said, "Let anyone among you who is without sin be the first to throw a stone at her" (John 8:7). As he spoke, his finger wrote some words in the dust. What the words were, we are not told. But seeing them, the mob of accusers quickly dispersed. Whereupon Jesus said to her, "Neither do I condemn you. Go your way, and from now on do not sin again." To all those caught in the web of sexual confusion and guilt, this is still the divine command.

Rebellion

You Can't Keep a Good Man (or Woman) Down

In Dr. Seuss' childhood classic, *How the Grinch Stole Christmas*, the author tells about the Grinch who hated Christmas and wanted to destroy it. Dr. Seuss says his heart was two sizes too small.

Jonah was a man like the Grinch. His heart was two sizes too small. And because it was, he refused to respond to God's call to service. He ran from God.

His story opens, "The word of the Lord came to Jonah." The exact manner in which it came is not clear. Jonah was told to go to Nineveh and warn that wicked city of God's impending doom. Judgment was hanging like a dark cloud over it, and God wanted it warned before it was too late.

Nineveh was the capital of Assyria, the ancient and dreadful enemy of Israel. The Assyrians were a cruel and barbaric military machine. Jonah, on the other hand, was a narrow, jealous, vindictive nationalist. He had bitter contempt and hatred for all the heathen world, especially the Assyrians. So instead of obeying God's call, he "set out to flee to Tarshish from the presence of the Lord" (Jon 1:3).

Tarshish was a mining port in Spain, a commercial outpost on the edge of civilization. Nineveh was 500 miles to the east of Israel. Tarshish was 2,000 miles to the west, at the end of the world in the other direction. It was as far from the call of God as Jonah could go.

At Joppa, Israel's chief seaport, Jonah found a ship preparing to sail for Tarshish. Any time you want to run from God, the devil will provide the transportation. So Jonah paid his fare and settled back with a sigh of relief.

Once out in the open seas the little ship was caught in a great storm. The Lord sent a screaming wind that ripped through its sails. Its timbers began to creak as it bobbed like a cork on the ocean. The mariners, accustomed to storms on the Mediterranean, would not be quickly frightened, but this was no ordinary blow. First they

Time out chair - the belly of the whale.

prayed. Then they began to cast the cargo overboard to lighten the ship. A lighter ship would ride the waves better. While the crew worked feverishly, Jonah was below deck, curled up in a warm place, fast asleep.

When the captain found Jonah, he awakened him and urged him to pray. At that moment Jonah was the only heathen on board. The crew became convinced that God was punishing them with the storm because of Jonah. Jonah drew the short straw or lot. He suggested, "Throw me into the sea; then the sea will quiet down" (1:12). He actually preferred death by drowning over obedience to God.

There was a nobility about these heathen mariners, for they did not want to throw Jonah overboard. With renewed zeal they tried to row the ship to shore. They cared more about Jonah than Jonah cared about Nineveh. When there was no other hope, they threw him into the sea.

The Lord had prepared a great fish, and as Jonah floated down to his watery grave, the fish swallowed him alive. For three days and three nights Jonah was in the belly of the fish.

This part of the story troubles some people. They say, "The only thing more ridiculous than the story of a fish swallowing a man is a man swallowing the story of a fish swallowing a man." Some even doubt that Jonah was a real person. They think of him as Hamlet or Macbeth, a fictitious character in a made-up story. The identity of Jonah as a historical person is not in question. According to 2 Kings 14:25, Jonah was not only a real person but an accredited prophet who lived in the village of Gath-hepher and prophesied during the reign of Jeroboam II, king of Israel, 785–745 B.C.

Was it a whale that swallowed Jonah? We don't know. The New Testament calls it a whale. But the Greek word should be translated "sea monster." The book of Jonah calls it "a large fish" (1:17).

Suddenly a whale house became a jail house, and from its belly Jonah prayed. Jonah had not prayed while the storm was raging. But now he said, "I called to the Lord out of my distress, and he answered me; out of the belly of sheol I cried, and you heard my voice" (2:2). "Sheol," the place of the dead, is the Hebrew word for "hell." The fish became a living tomb for Jonah. That's why our Lord used Jonah's experience as an illustration of his own. He said, "As Jonah was three days and three nights in the belly of the sea monster, so for three days and three nights the Son of Man will be in the heart of the earth" (Matt 12:40).

Then Jonah said, "As my life was ebbing away I remembered the Lord" (2:7). Jonah turned the belly of the fish into an altar to God. For three days and three nights he cried to God: "God, save me. Get me out of here, and I will do whatever you want me to do."

Sound familiar? That's the way we all do. When things are going well with us—when we have health, a good job, plenty to eat, and a fine home—we are all self-made. But when tragedy strikes, God is the first one we cry out to.

Have you ever been where Jonah was? Have you ever prayed, "Lord, if you will . . . restore my health . . . preserve my marriage . . . save my child . . . get me out of this financial crisis . . . help me find a job . . . give me the ability to pass this exam . . . I will serve you the rest of my life"?

Jonah was ready to obey God. So the Lord released him from the great fish onto dry land. Rescued from the sea and fish, Jonah was again called to be God's messenger to Nineveh (3:1-2). This time Jonah obeyed. His preaching was cold and heartless. There was no tear in his eye, no ache in his heart, no pathos in his voice. The preaching was effective. Everyone repented and turned to God, even the king.

Nowhere do we read in the Bible or outside of it that one message from a servant of the Lord was used by God to so great an extent. The whole city of Nineveh believed God! Nothing remotely approximating that great a conversion has ever taken place in the history of revivals.

When Nineveh repented, God repented. When the people turned from their sin, God turned from judgment. The whole city was saved.

If someone unaided by the spirit of God had written this story, it probably would have concluded at this point. You would think that this great revival would have pleased Jonah, but he was angry with God. The word angry means "to burn within." Jonah resented the fact that God had spared the city. He was bitter toward God and wanted to die.

Jonah had obeyed the Lord in going to Nineveh and preaching God's message, but his attitude had not changed. He so hated the Ninevehites for their cruelty that deep within his heart he had looked forward to their destruction. He adopted an "I told you so" attitude. He prayed,

> Oh, Lord! Is this not what I said while I was still in my own country? That is why I fled before to Tarshish at the beginning: for I knew that you are a gracious God and merciful, slow to anger, and abounding in steadfast love, and ready to relent from punishing. (4:2)

For the first time Jonah revealed why he ran from God. It was not out of fear of failure, but out of fear of success. He knew what God was like. God had the welfare of all people upon His heart, and passionately desired to lift them from their sin. Jonah did not share that love. He had only contempt and hatred for the heathen world. His heart was two sizes too small. He had no sorrow over Nineveh's lostness, and likewise no joy over its salvation.

In the final passage of the book God presents a challenge to Jonah in a dramatic form in an enacted parable. Jonah went outside the city and sat under a small shed to see what might happen to the city. The Lord made a gourd, a large leafy plant, to grow and provide a much needed shade for Jonah. This pleased him very much. The next day, however, a worm ate into the gourd, and it withered and died. Jonah blazed with anger because his shade was gone.

The Lord then suggested that if Jonah had compassion on a worthless gourd to whose existence he had contributed nothing, he should see some grounds for the Lord having compassion on the 120,000 inhabitants of Nineveh. The Lord asked,

Should I not be concerned about Nineveh, that great city in which there are more than a hundred and twenty thousand persons who do not know their right hand from their left, and also many animals? (4:11)

The question that forms the climax of the book is really the message of the book: God loves all people and wants to deal with them in mercy and kindness. It is his very nature to do so. We should expect it of him. We see, then, in this little book of forty-eight verses, the high-water mark of the Old Testament's teachings about God's universal love. And the universal love of God forms the Old Testament basis for all missions.

The book of Jonah, therefore, is the greatest missionary book in the Old Testament. In it there are three great truths on exclusiveness and spiritual indifference.

God Loves Everyone

God loves all people and wants them to be saved. This universal love forms the basis for world missions. In the story of Jonah, God loved Israel, the chosen people, but God also loved Assyria, the enemy of Israel. God loves all people and is concerned that we love them, too, that our hearts stay warm and tender toward them.

F. B. Meyer, the famous British preacher, reportedly once spent a night as a house guest of A. B. Simpson, founder of the Christian and Missionary Alliance. Early the next morning Meyer strolled downstairs, thinking he was the first one up.

But no, there through the partially opened door to the study he could see Mr. Simpson in prayer. He had a world globe in front of him, and he would put his finger on a spot and pray. Then he would spin it, put his finger on another spot, and pray. Then, as F. B. Meyer watched unnoticed, A. B. Simpson leaned forward and took the whole globe in his arms, hugged it and wept. That's the big heart of God.

We Are Called To Go

Because God loves everyone, God calls us to share the gospel with the lost world. As the word of the Lord came to Jonah, so it comes to us. Jesus said, "Come to me all you that are weary and carrying heavy burdens, and I will give you rest" (Matt 11:28). No sooner do we come to the Savior than we hear him say,

> Go therefore, and make disciples of all nations, baptizing them in the name of the Father and of the Son and of the Holy Spirit, teaching them to obey everything I have commanded you. And remember, I am with you always, even to the end of the age. (28:19-20)

We must go and share the good news of salvation with the lost world. How else shall people know that God is gracious? How else shall they know of God's willingness to forgive and to save?

We are called to be a part of extending the glory of God. We do that by telling others of the Lord. If we go and tell, people will believe and repent.

Sharing Is Voluntary

Even though God calls us to go and tell, the divine summons can be resisted. The prophets were not mere machines, and neither are we. We are living beings who must consent to do God's will. We must bow our wills to God's will voluntarily.

In every generation and in every congregation there are some people who, like Jonah, fail to see God's larger purpose and program and do not share God's compassion for the world. It is because their hearts, like the heart of Jonah, are two sizes too small. They are narrow and exclusive.

At the end of Dr. Seuss' story the Grinch experienced an amazing growth in his heart. It grew three sizes, and he enjoyed

Christmas like everyone else. I pray that our hearts will grow equal to the heart of God in caring about a lost world.

Every one of us needs to ask, "Oh, God, is there any of the spirit of Jonah in me? Is my heart so small that I cannot see the Ninevehites around me?"

* * * * *

This book may have fallen into the hands of some modern-day Jonah. You are reading it on your way to a distant Tarshish. May I remind you that when you run from God, you are likely to run into an unforgettable storm. Your best hope is to stop running from God and start running to and then with God. God is offering you a second chance in God's service. Take it now. Forget about the big fish. Look at the big heart of God. Then hear and answer the divine call. Saying yes to God is the end to strife and the beginning of life.